# ASPECTS of PSYCHOLOGY RESEARCH METHODS and STATISTICS

# RESEARCH
# METHODS
# and STATISTICS

## HUGH COOLICAN

Hodder & Stoughton

A MEMBER OF THE HODDER HEADLINE GROUP

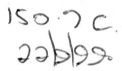

*British Library Cataloguing in Publication Data*
A catalogue record for this title is available from the British Library

ISBN 0 340 74899 0

First published 1999
Impression number    10  9  8  7  6  5  4  3  2  1
Year    2003  2002  2001  2000  1999

Typeset by GreenGate Publishing Services, Tonbridge, Kent.
Printed and bound in Great Britain for Hodder and Stoughton Educational, a division of
Hodder Headline plc, 338 Euston Road, London NW1 3BH,
by Cox & Wyman, Reading, Berks

# CONTENTS

# PREFACE

The *Aspects of Psychology* series aims to provide a short and concise, but detailed and highly accessible, account of selected areas of psychological theory and research.

This book is not about what psychologists have discovered or investigated. It is about how psychological investigations are conducted and how psychologists can be sure that they are discovering causes of, and influences on, human behaviour and experience in an objective and scientific manner. The methods of psychologists must be transparent and their data must be publicly accessible in order for us to be able to agree that their findings are reliable and valid.

Most psychology courses ask students to acquire some of the methods and data analysis techniques of the researcher so that they will appreciate that the findings they read about are not fanciful and that they are achieved through thorough modes of investigation. Here you will learn what is a real experiment, how hypotheses are tested, what is a psychological measurement, how people should be interviewed, what are the problems involved in observing people, and how psychologists eliminate different variables as explanations of what affects our behaviour. Finally you will learn how to handle data (numbers or text) and how to report your findings. These skills are extremely useful in life even if you never study psychology again – but of course I hope you will!

For the purposes of revision, I have included detailed summaries of the material presented in each chapter. Instead of a separate glossary, for easy reference the Index contains page numbers in bold which refer to definitions and main explanations of particular concepts.

# ACKNOWLEDGEMENTS

Thanks to Richard Gross and Rob McIlveen for their comments and support in producing this volume in the Aspects series. Thanks especially to Greig Aitken for endless support and patience with deadlines. Thanks also to Tim Gregson-Williams, and to Anna Churchman and Dave Mackin at GreenGate Publishing.

Index compiled by Frank Merrett, Cheltenham, Gloucester.

# OVERVIEW OF PSYCHOLOGICAL RESEARCH METHODS, THEIR USES AND ETHICAL IMPLICATIONS

## Introduction

This chapter introduces you to the most common methods used in psychological research. First we consider how psychologists attempt to develop explanations of human behaviour using the traditional thinking of the natural sciences, in which theories are proposed, and predictions that follow from the theories (hypotheses) are tested. The results of these tests determine whether each theory is supported or challenged. Such testing must use careful measurement of variables and well controlled research designs. The chapter then summarises the strengths, weaknesses and rationale for several methods within this tradition, such as the experiment, interview, questionnaire and direct observation and includes a brief review of related ethical issues.

## Why do psychological research?

Psychologists are often telephoned by the media and asked to tell listeners or readers how they should discipline their children, how they can stop eating too much or how to give up smoking. No psychological researcher worth their salt will give a simple answer to such questions. Unlike politicians, this is not because they do not *want* to give a straight answer, but because they know there *are* no simple answers to such complex issues. What psychologists *can* do is report the findings of research studies that investigate differences between, say, physically punished children and those not physically punished. Physically punished children are often more aggressive, for instance. However, psychologists will not necessarily say from this that you should not physically punish your children. Nor will they say that physical punishment is therefore *proven* to cause aggressiveness. All that can be said is that they have found a relationship and that the theory that physical punishment is part of the cause of some forms of aggression is *supported.*

## The hypothesis testing approach

Psychological researchers seek *evidence* to support theories about human behaviour and this is something like the way in which detectives seek evidence to support the prosecution of criminals. Rarely is a criminal *proven* to have committed a crime; juries mostly decide on the balance of probability. Similarly, researchers seek *empirical data* which will *support* an existing theory about human behaviour and experience, or which will lead to a new theory. We do not *prove* theories true – we *support* them with findings from data.

Let us suppose that the psychology tutors at Learnwell College believe that a healthy lifestyle improves students' chances of academic success. They define 'healthy lifestyle' in a way which includes good sleep and regular exercise. We would call their belief a *theory* about human behaviour. How might the tutors go about supporting their theory? Well, if the theory is correct we can make certain predictions from it. A *prediction from a theory about what we expect to find in the world is known as a* **hypothesis**.

---

**PAUSE FOR THOUGHT**

What hypotheses might our tutors make? What specific predictions could they make from their theory that a healthy lifestyle leads to better examination grades?

---

Well, if good sleep improves academic performance we can make a hypothesis that, *all other things being equal,* a group of students who sleep well will obtain better exam grades than a group who have bad sleep patterns. Of course we should then have to define:

● good sleep;
● better exam grades;
● all other things being equal.

and there is a lot tied up in this last phrase which we shall discuss in Chapter 3. For the moment, what we mean is that the students should be much the same in all important respects, except for their sleep patterns. What then do we mean by 'good sleep'?

## Variables

Psychologists (and all other scientists), study relationships between *variables*. A variable is any property which can change, such as temperature, length of grass, aggressive behaviour or level of anxiety. Of course, temperature is easier to assess than level of aggressiveness. However, such levels certainly do change and it is the psychologist's job to relate these changes to other variables or events such as level of frustration or the environmental circumstances under which aggression is more likely to appear.

Students often think their tutors are splitting hairs over exact definitions. However, if we do not make clear definitions we cannot engage in the open activity of scientific research. If someone claims to have found a connection between sleep quality and exam grades we might well want to check out their claim. If they will not or cannot tell us what they meant by 'good sleep', we cannot attempt to *replicate* what they have done. *Replication* of a study refers to an attempt to obtain the same result as did a previous researcher, using an almost identical method and procedure.

## Operational definitions

In scientific research exact definitions of variables are often referred to as *operational definitions*. These are precise definitions of a variable in terms of the procedures taken to measure it. Suppose we define 'good sleep' as eight hours or more per night, with no break. Few people get this *every* night so we might add the criterion that students qualify for the 'good sleep' group if they get this much sleep at least five nights out of every seven on average. This now tells other researchers what our criteria were for identifying students as good sleepers. It is the operational definition of good sleep used in our study. It may not be every-one's everyday definition of good sleep but it makes the conduct of our research study very clear to other researchers. 'Bad sleep' in our study might be defined as five hours or less. The other operational definition needed is that of 'academic success' in terms of higher exam grades. Exam grades are already clearly defined, so here we may only have to turn letters into numbers, for instance 10 for an A grade, 8 for a B grade and so on.

## Research hypotheses

Once we have carefully defined our variables we can turn the generally worded hypothesis above into a specific *research hypothesis*.

'We expect students having an average of eight hours' or more unbroken sleep per night to obtain higher exam grades than do students getting an average of five hours' sleep per night or less.'

A research hypothesis states exactly what is expected to happen in terms of differences or relationships between variables. By the time a research hypothesis is made, the variables must be explic-itly and carefully defined in operational terms. Hence, accepting that we have already precisely defined 'good sleep' and 'bad sleep', we could simply say that we expect those with good sleep patterns to have higher exam grades than those with bad sleep patterns.

## Research designs

What we now have is a rough outline for a *research design* to test our research hypothesis. We have defined good and bad sleep groups and we have defined the variables we shall measure. We would need to go on to specify exactly *who* we would study (our *sample* of students), and exactly *how* we obtain the sleep pattern information from them.

## The nature of data and 'facts'

A research design is a method for gathering *empirical data* with which to test a hypothesis or develop a theory. Empirical data are (note 'data' is plural) bits of information which we obtain from observation of the external world. They are not claims about the world, nor theories, nor intuitions nor hunches. If researchers are doing their job properly, data are objective recordings of happenings in the world. By 'objective' we mean that the researcher has tried very hard not to let their own preconceived views and prejudices influence the recording of the data. In effect any other honest researcher should record pretty well exactly the same events in the same way if they were in the same position. We may not agree that Jenny is 'nervous' but we can easily agree on how often she taps her fingers or bites her lips. This is publicly observable behaviour; being nervous is an *inference* we often make *from* such data.

At a very basic level, empirical data are facts, though we must be very careful with the term 'fact'. For instance, is it a fact that your brother Rob is boisterous? He may appear to be by your family's standards and from your perspective, but he may appear quite reserved by comparison with his friends. To a naïve child a stick appears bent in water. Is the man wobbling towards you really drunk? We cannot describe this as a fact. What we can report is that he wobbles, lurches, talks incoherently and has a bottle of whiskey in his hand. He could nevertheless be acting or ill.

In the preceding example a positive result for our hypothesis relating sleep and exam success would indicate **support** for our theory, not proof. In fact, 'proof' is a term to be avoided in talking about theories, hypotheses and research for the simple reason that there are always several possible alternative explanations for any findings. In all sciences, not just psychology, theories are proposed, then supported. Other scientists usually propose alternative explanations and try to establish these.

---

**PAUSE FOR THOUGHT**

What factor, *other than lack of sleep*, might be responsible for the students with less sleep getting lower examination grades?

---

To take our example again, it may be that those students who get little sleep also tend to be those who do extra paid work in the evenings or who stay out partying. It might be for these reasons that they do less well in their studies. This is the sort of complication behind the phrase 'all other things being equal' (page 2).

### Science as open argument

However, suppose lack of sleep really does lead directly to poor study performance. Even if our research leads to this conclusion, we still do not yet know *why* this is so. Facts alone will not help us to understand or develop theories. Facts are used by researchers in an *argument* about explanations. It is these arguments that are the heart of scientific progress and it is the way that findings are used in arguments that leads to the survival of one theory about the world in preference to another. It is this construction of argument, provision of support with publicly accessible data, and willingness to consider alternative explanations, that make a subject scientific. Without these, psychologists would not be engaged in a valid form of investigation or a genuine search for understanding. Who else makes statements about human behaviour? Astrologers, religious leaders and charlatans selling you a course in business success, to mention a few. None of these engage in empirical research, basing their theory directly on the findings.

The role of research in psychology is to make it an objective, scientific study, rather than 'armchair philosophy'. Compared with armchair astrology or religious explanation, the claims psychologists make about human behaviour and experience have to be supported with evidence. This book is about how to gather and analyse that evidence, honestly, effectively and efficiently.

# Theory generation and descriptive approaches

Not all psychological research is about testing hypotheses, though much of it is. Suppose we are interested in an area of cross-cultural research (see page 47) where we wish to explore differing concepts of emotion in an Eastern and Western industrialised society (e.g. Japan and the UK). Here we might conduct an exploratory study, where we simply gather and categorise data from samples living in the two societies until we can begin to see a clear pattern emerging. Descriptive studies are those which *describe* what they observe in a research setting without necessarily moving on to the creation of theory, though this is often a subsequent aim. Studies can also aim to *generate* theories rather than to test them. A lot of Pavlov's early studies, for instance, were simply exploring the circumstances under which conditioned reflexes could be obtained.

# Quantitative and qualitative approaches

*Quantitative data* are numerical in form. They are the sort of thing we have already mentioned in connection with operational definitions. They are the data we acquire when we *measure* things and they are very common in the natural sciences. *Qualitative data* are *meanings*, very often language in the form in which it was originally produced by a research participant when asked a question. If you ask me to rate my confidence in the current prime minister on a scale of one to ten you will receive quantitative data. If you ask me to describe my feelings about the current prime minister's competence you will receive some qualitative data. You can of course attempt to convert my qualitative data in to a quantitative form by rating or coding the content of what I say (see page 153) into certain categories.

Researchers using qualitative methods very often take a theory generation or descriptive approach to data gathering whereas quantitative work is very often directed towards the testing of hypotheses. However, this division is by no means universal. Some quantitative work is descriptive (e.g. the development of a scale to measure aggressiveness) and some qualitative work can test hypotheses (see Hayes, 1997, Chapter 6).

# Getting to grips with research methods

We often find that psychology students love the theories but dislike the research methods. This is unfortunate since we cannot have the theories without the research work that goes into establishing them! We cannot get excited over Milgram's astonishing obedience work (Milgram 1974), or the physiological basis of emotions, without someone first doing the research upon which the theories rest. A theory without supportive research is rather like a criminal's story with no alibi. It *may* be true but why on earth should we believe it in preference to any other story? The good thing about completing a research methods course in psychology, is that it can develop your critical powers. Whenever you encounter a politician's or advertiser's claim in the media you should find yourself saying 'I wonder what evidence they base that on?', 'How on earth could they support that idea?', and so on. Even when evidence *is* presented you become able to see that the interpretation based on the evidence is not the only possible explanation. For example, the fact that physically punished children are more aggressive does not *prove* that hitting children *causes* them to become aggressive. It is a strong possibility, but another possible interpretation is that parents who use physical punishment *also* tend to encourage aggression. How do we decide between these two alternatives? More research is needed.

A second benefit of a research methods course is that you get to go out and actually gather data, investigate results and speculate about what you might have shown and what further investigations could be made.

# Forms of investigation

Let us now think about the types of investigation the Learnwell College tutors might devise. We know they can record the exam results easily enough but how will they identify the groups of students getting over eight hours' sleep per night and five or less hours' sleep per night?

---

**PAUSE FOR THOUGHT**

Try to think of specific procedures that the tutors might use in order to be able to measure the difference between two groups of students, one getting 'good sleep' according to our criteria, and one getting 'bad sleep', in terms of exam grades.

---

The tutors could use any of the general methods outlined below in Box 1.1 (and perhaps a few more):

---

**Box 1.1** *Procedures for identifying samples of 'good sleep' and 'bad sleep' students*

| Procedure to identify 'good sleep' and 'bad sleep' students | General method: |
|---|---|
| 1 Ask students how they have slept during the academic year. | interview/questionnaire |
| 2 Put cameras into student bedrooms and record sleeping and waking times. | observation |
| 3 Ask students to keep a diary from the beginning of the year. | (self) observation |
| 4 Ask for volunteers and allocate one group to having five hours' sleep or less and another group to having eight hours' sleep a night for three weeks; participants then sit mini-exam. | experiment |

---

Methods 1 and 3 look promising but methods 2 and 4 seem to involve some serious ethical issues and we shall discuss these later in this chapter. For now, note that all the major investigative methods that psychological researchers use are listed above (though there are many approaches within each category). Apart from using existing records (such as census data) psychology researchers seeking information about human behaviour must either ask questions, observe people directly, or conduct experiments. It is the last of these that we shall now address.

## The role of the experiment – the manipulation of variables

When people hear that in psychology we conduct experiments they often jump to the worrying conclusion that psychologists manipulate people. Actually, the things we attempt to manipulate in experiments are *variables*, and this is no different from any other experimental science. The trouble is that the variables are often aspects of human behaviour, such as the recall of text or solving a problem.

To recognise the essential components of an experiment, you may recall the typical science class during which a piece of metal was heated by a Bunsen burner while students took regular measurements of its temperature and its length. In this example we varied the temperature of the metal and *observed* the consequent change in length. The manipulated variable is always known as the *independent variable* whilst the observed variable (assumed to be changing as a result of changes in the independent variable) is known as the *dependent variable*. Notice that it might be naive to use a metal rule to measure the length of the piece of metal. The heat is likely to expand the rule itself, giving us an inaccurate measure of true length and thus *confounding* our results. If we ran the sleep and exam performance experiment described in Box 1, we might find that it is not the lower sleep level that is responsible for a poorer exam performance, but the extra activities the students were able to participate in that caused the difference. Extra alcohol consumption, for instance, might be a *confounding variable*.

- In an experiment we manipulate an *independent variable* whilst holding all other variables constant and measuring any change in a *dependent variable*.
- Variables which systematically affect the dependent variable are known as *confounding variables*.
- *Random errors* are any other non-systematic effects which interfere with accurate data collection on our variables.

### Rationale of the experiment – determining cause and effect

The logic of the experiment is fairly clear: if we hold everything constant and vary only one thing (the independent variable) then any change in a related dependent variable must be caused by the changes in the independent variable. This is the logic we employ in day-to-day situations such as trying to identify the cause of interference on our television. If we suspect that an electrical appliance is causing the interference we turn each appliance off, one at a time, until the interference stops. This should identify the offending appliance so long as we do not have one of those nasty complications, such as when interference only occurs when both the food mixer *and* the oven are turned on at the same. In reality, situations are usually at least this complicated whether in psychology or any other science, but in starting to look at scientific method it is simplest to start considering only one variable at a time.

### A typical psychology experiment

Suppose your class group decides to conduct the following experiment on conformity. You wish to check out the notion that people are more likely to drop litter if they see that others have already done so. In an empty room with one desk but no bin, each participant is given a packet of crisps to eat and then handed a task to perform which entails them clearing the desk in front of them. We observe whether participants drop the crisp packet on the floor or dispose of it 'tidily' (putting it in their pockets or handing it to the experimenter). In one condition there are already three crisp packets lying on the floor. In another condition there are initially no crisp packets on the floor.

**PAUSE FOR THOUGHT**

What do you think is the independent variable and the dependent variable in the experiment just described?

What would be the independent variable and dependent variable in the sleep comparison experiment described earlier in this chapter?

The *independent variable* manipulated in this experiment is the number of crisp packets that we initially leave lying on the floor when the participant starts their trial. Our dependent variable is whether or not participants drop their crisp packet on the floor. If they do drop more in the three packet condition we can conclude that the presence of the packets on the floor influenced participants' packet dropping. In the sleep comparison experiment, the independent variable is the number of hours' sleep and the dependent variable is the mini exam grade.

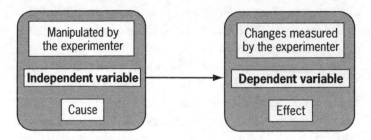

**Figure 1.1** *The independent and dependent variable in an experiment*

In Chapter 2 we shall return to these experiments and investigate their strengths and weaknesses. For now, let us just note that a tiny difference between conditions in the number of packets dropped would not be adequate support for the conclusion that the independent variable had an effect, nor would a tiny exam grade difference. We usually want the differences to be quite large and this is the subject of *statistical significance testing* covered in Chapter 5.

### Advantages and disadvantages of experiments

**Advantages:** The fundamental strength of a true experiment is its power in leading us to a cause–effect relationship. In addition, we know before we can possibly run an experiment that our independent variable and dependent variable must be carefully and operationally defined, otherwise we should not (usually) start to run the experiment. In non-experimental studies it is possible to gather large quantities of data and then find that the wrong questions have been asked or that there is no way to adequately quantify the variables under research.

**Disadvantages:** Because we must tightly define and control our variables it can be that experiments lack a degree of realism. For instance, psychologists often test memory using long word lists, yet rarely in everyday use of memory would people need to use this ability. In our proposed sleep-study experiment, to what extent is a three-week sleep pattern likely to affect performance in the way that would occur with a regular pattern, maintained over an academic year? To what extent would students work for, and worry over, an exam which they know is only experimental? We have raised here the problem of *validity* which we shall return to on page 43. For now, note that Carlsmith, Elsworth & Aronson (1976) talked of two kinds of realism – *mundane* and *experimental. Mundane realism* asks to what degree the experimental environment and design mimic real life. *Experimental realism* occurs where the experimental procedures, though lacking a relationship with 'everyday life', nevertheless are so gripping that participants' behaviour is still genuine and wholehearted. Such situations occurred in the Milgram (1974) obedience studies and in those of Latané & Darley (1976) where participants had to intervene when research assistants or fellow participants appeared to be in genuine distress.

If we were to attempt to make the sleep-study experiment realistic we would have to ask students to have five hours' sleep per night for the whole academic year. This raises certain ethical problems. Thus a second disadvantage of 'true' experiments is that they often throw up serious ethical implications stemming from the control of conditions, variables and behaviour that is required. Ethical issues are discussed in Box 1.2 (page 24). Even in a three-week experiment we might encounter particular problems of mental and physical threat to participants and we could even create some knock-on effect in the continuation of their studies. Ethical considerations often rule out research designs which, on a purely logical basis, would give us strong evidence on an issue of debate within psychology. It is simply not acceptable to rear some children in poor families and some in rich ones, in order to estimate the different effects that such environments have on a growing child's intellectual abilities!

# Major methods in non-experimental studies

To some extent, certain versions of the major non-experimental methods described here can also lack realism (for instance, interviewing people about how they might react to the Milgram situation) but most tend to be closer to everyday behaviour and attitudes. On the other hand, they tend to suffer proportionately more from a lack of clarity about causes and effects than experimental methods.

## Asking people questions

In order to discover how students have slept over the past year we could simply ask them about it. Psychologists have several methods for asking questions and gathering *self-report* data from participants. Researchers can:

- conduct a face-to-face interview;
- administer a questionnaire as part of an interview;
- administer questionnaires to large groups in person, by post or phone.

In each case, various types of question can be asked.

### *Open or closed questions*

If we ask an *open* question such as:

a 'Tell me about your typical sleep pattern over the past year'

we will obtain qualitative data from the participant. This will need analysis; various methods of analysis for qualitative data are described in Chapter 6.

Historically, the majority of psychological researchers have preferred to gather quantitative data in order to make statistical comparisons. Partly for this reason, many questions have tended to be *closed* – meaning that only a certain range of answers are possible, very often leading to a numerical score on a scale. For instance, we can ask:

b 'Please estimate the average number of hours sleep you have had each night over the past year'

or to give other examples:

c 'Please state your eating habits':
   vegan    vegetarian    meat-eating    other (please specify)

d 'Do you often feel anxious for no particular reason?'
   yes/no

e 'Please rate your feeling of anxiety now, compared with your normal state, on the scale below'

   much less anxious                           much more anxious
   than normal                                 than normal
   0 _____ 100

f 'Children should not be physically punished'
   strongly agree    agree    undecided    disagree    strongly disagree

Note that items c and d will give us data in *categories* whereas items b, e and f provide us with a number or position along a scale (see page 73). This is important in terms of the kinds of statistical analysis we can perform on the data gathered so you should always think what you will want to *do* with your data finally before launching out with the questionnaire you have created for a research project.

## *Interviews*

*Structured* interviews do not differ much from the use of a questionnaire, except that the questionnaire is used while the researcher is in one-to-one contact with the *respondent* (the term given to a participant who answers a questionnaire). *Surveys* consist of administering a questionnaire to a large sample of respondents, usually using a fairly structured procedure.

*Semi-structured* interviews are probably the most frequently used type in contemporary psychological research. Here the idea is to ask a pre-arranged set of questions but to attempt to make the interview situation unthreatening and relaxed for the interviewee. The aim is to extract as much genuine and detailed information from the interviewee as possible. Unlike the formal interview or questionnaire design, in the semi-structured interview the interviewee is free to talk for as long as they wish and to include whatever detail they think important. The interviewer asks questions in the most natural order possible, given the flow of conversation, and does not ask at all where the participant happens to volunteer appropriate information before a scheduled question has been put. It is the researcher's job to analyse these qualitative data at a later stage and to extract from them whatever information was required of the investigation. We shall discuss the collection and analysis of such data in Chapter 6. See also Smith (1995) for a useful guide to the procedures used in semi-structured interviewing and also for a useful guide to analysis of data and subsequent report writing.

### *Advantages and disadvantages of the interview method*

**Advantages:** Compared with most methods, the interview allows us to get at the meanings intended by participants. Questionnaires restrict participants to only the items given and often to a narrow set of possible responses. Observation, as we shall see, will often permit the gathering of only predetermined categories of visible behaviour. Very formal interviews differ little in their strengths and weaknesses from questionnaires (see page 65) except that even here the interviewer is able to clarify questions and perhaps put the participant at ease in terms of their behaviour being *evaluated* (see page 60). The semi-structured interview approach, however, is highly flexible. The interviewer may pick up on ideas not predicted by other methods and any ambiguities in questions can be explored. Participants can explain that they do not understand a question and the interviewer can rephrase it. The interviewer can also check the participant's understanding and even follow up lines of questioning that were not originally planned for, thus adding to the scope of the original aims of the study.

**Disadvantages:** The less controlled interview suffers from the weaknesses shared with most methods which gather open-ended, qualitative data. Where the aim is to measure variables fairly precisely, this method provides data which must be operationalised at a later stage. Since participants have been treated differently in their interviews, their responses will also vary in type, and researchers have the problem of assessing these data on a similar basis. This means that assessments made may be inconsistent and *unreliable* (see page 66), making comparisons difficult. If the interviewer is also the person who assesses the data, all sorts of biases can enter the process because the interviewer may have certain expectations, from personal experience with the interviewee, that leads to 'reading into' the data what is not actually there. The interviewer is not detached; we shall discuss strategies for dealing with this sort of bias in Chapter 3.

The provision of a structured question and response system, as in a questionnaire, can help participants find answers, whereas in an interview situation some may find it hard to think of anything appropriate to say. Finally, where the interview session is conducted on a fairly informal basis, the influence of interpersonal variables, such as liking or disliking between interviewer and interviewee, can have significant distorting effects on the data obtained. Such effects are also discussed in Chapter 3.

On a purely practical basis, individual interviews take a lot more time to administer than do some forms of questionnaire or survey where several people can be asked to complete a form at the same time and no conversation is permitted.

## Observation

All research entails observation; scientists observe their instruments to record data. When we refer to an observational approach, however, we do not refer to the observation of instruments, nor to the recording of predetermined categories of behaviour as in an experiment (e.g. did the subject drop a crisp packet or not?). Nor do we refer to the observation of responses to questionnaires or in an interview. An *observational approach* refers only to direct viewing and recording of behaviour as it happens or happened, freely, in a relatively unconstrained environment. This definition includes the observation of behaviour previously recorded on video tape.

Where psychologists record behaviour as it happens, in an everyday environment for the person observed, the approach is referred to as *naturalistic observation*, as is also the case for studies of various animals in their own natural habitat.

Even though the behaviour observed is freely produced, the method for assessing it can be structured to a lesser or greater extent. In qualitative studies the emphasis is on broad and detailed description of the totality of behaviour produced in a given context. In *structured* observation studies, though behaviour may be wide-ranging, only a behaviour in a predetermined set of categories is recorded for later analysis.

### Structured observation

For instance, in a structured observation study of children's social development, researchers might observe children in a playroom and record only patterns of interaction which can be classed as 'co-operative'. Such patterns will have been clearly defined before observation starts and might include such incidents as:

- gives toy to another on request with no protest;
- joins in game and plays according to rules;
- joins another to work jointly on same task.

Observers will code behaviour by using a coding check-sheet, part of which might appear as shown in Figure 1.2.

| Child | Time | | Joins in play with rules | Works on joint task | Gives toy – no protest | ... | ... |
|-------|------|-----|--------------------------|---------------------|------------------------|-----|-----|
| | From: | to: | | | | | |
| A | 10.05 | 10.11 | X | | | | |
| | 10.12 | 10.14 | | X | | | |
| | 10.15 | | | | X | | |

**Figure 1.2** *Possible part of behaviour coding sheet for observers assessing 'co-operative' behaviour in children at play*

## Qualitative observation

On the other hand, a qualitative researcher studying social inter-action in a business office might take notes on all interactions which occur and attempt to categorise these later using one of the methods described in Chapter 6.

## Participant observation

A further distinction between observation studies is possible. The observer (researcher) can be external to the group and just watch it, or act as a member (participant) of the group. Rachel (1996), for instance, attempted to follow organisational change in a computer systems design office. She looked particularly at relationships between a 'systems team' and a 'change manage-ment team'. She discusses the difficulty of being two things at once, a working group participant *and* an observer of those with whom one is working:

> 'The skill then becomes that of finding a way to ... maintain oneself as a member of an academic community while opening oneself up to the possibilities that would follow from belonging to the community that one wants to study.' (Rachel, 1996, page 115)

## Disclosure

This neatly brings up a serious technical and ethical issue. To what extent does it matter whether people are *aware* that they are being observed? In Chapter 3 we discuss the issue of *participant reactivity* and *expectancy* – the extent to which knowing that one is being studied affects the way in which one behaves. However, if a researcher wishes to avoid any such effects and therefore observes people without their knowledge, we run into the ethi-cal issues of consent and invasion of privacy. When would this matter and when not? It would seem fairly harmless to observe people as they cross a busy street, noting the extent to which they break traffic rules, the extent to which the presence of oth-ers inhibits or facilitates this behaviour, the manner in which people break rules and so on. This behaviour would have occurred anyway and is already public. However, where people are observed in an office by a researcher who is posing as a regular employee, then they may disclose information or behave in ways they would not want recorded and published in a research paper. The researcher must respect such privacy rights and do at least one of the following things:

- ensure anonymity for those observed;
- disclose own identity and ask for permission before writing up the report;
- give finished material to those who are obviously identified to see whether they approve of publication of the report.

### *Intervention*

Another observational design possibility incurring ethical concerns is that in which some kind of *intervention* occurs before observations are made. Researchers might hand out leaflets (see Cialdini, 1990, page 37), stop a car to see how many people hoot at it, ask directions or fall down apparently sick or drunk (as in Piliavin, Rodin & Piliavin, 1969). Here again, the researchers must think very carefully about their responsibilities to the profession of psychology and to the rights of members of the general public.

### *Advantages and disadvantages of observation studies*

Since observational studies vary very widely in type it is difficult to summarise for all types of study. Here we concentrate simply on the contrast between methods involving the observation of free-flowing behaviour and those where the participant responds to an interviewer, questionnaire or experimenter.

**Advantages:** Observed behaviour is continuous, not a simple response to an artificial or unfamiliar stimulus (as in many experiments). Situations can be studied which are not amenable to experiment or to the use of questioning (e.g. work with young children or animals; skilled behaviour where questions would break concentration; behaviour which is difficult to report about oneself, such as social interactions, eye contact, decision making in groups). Where people are unaware of being observed, behaviour is genuine, without effects from expectancy (see page 59) or from the interaction between researcher and participant.

**Disadvantages:** Behaviour may be difficult to record accurately; different observers may disagree about what they have recorded (see reliability on page 66). Where people are aware of being observed their behaviour may alter as a result. Ethical issues arise where people are unaware of being observed. It may be difficult anyway for observers to remain undisclosed, or to hide their equipment, and once people's suspicions are aroused the nature of the study may change radically. Variables are poorly controlled compared with an experimental situation and therefore there is greater room for observers to be biased in what they record. The greater the variability in the observing situation the harder it will be for anyone to replicate the study's findings exactly.

### Questions and observation as techniques within experiments

It should be noted here that psychologists can use observation, questionnaires and interviews as part of an overall experimental design. Bandura, for instance, in his well known studies demonstrating children's modelling of adult aggressive behaviour, used observation to measure the dependent variable (aggressive responses) in many of his studies (e.g. Bandura, 1965). Interviews can be used to assess people's levels of frustration after attempting difficult problems, and many studies use questionnaires to measure people's moods or states of anxiety after participating in an experiment.

## Case studies

Many research investigations in psychology have been in the form of case studies where a single individual or group is studied in depth, often over an extended period of time. Cases of interest might be a person with specific brain damage which causes particular forms of memory problem, a person with an unusual form of psychological disturbance or groups studied using participant observation, such as a street gang or religious cult group. The study itself usually involves a series of detailed observations, interviews and perhaps tests in which a mass of both quantitative and qualitative data is gathered.

### Advantages and disadvantages of case studies

**Advantage:** we obtain rich and genuine qualitative data from case studies which might produce the exception that disproves a general rule or which might generate a whole spectrum of new, more quantitative research on larger groups of not-so-special people. We also obtain a unique view that could not be obtained from studies on larger numbers of 'normal' people.

**Disadvantages:** include the fact that such a detailed study can probably not be replicated in its entirety and that there is often no one to check the observations, interpretations and selections of the single researcher who worked with the particular case. In addition, it is possible that the deep involvement of the researcher with the particular person studied may have an effect on what that person experiences and reports. In the case of mental disturbance, such involvement may well have a bearing on the person's rate and form of recovery.

## Ethics in research

Researchers in psychology are bound by the code of practice of their professional organisations – the British Psychological Society in the UK, the American Psychological Association in the USA, and equivalent organisations in most other countries where psychology is researched and practised. Some texts contain detailed discussions of the principles involved (e.g. Coolican, 1996, 1999; Gross & McIlveen, 1999). However, the reader should note that the main motivation towards behaving ethically towards research participants should not be because one is bound by an organisation's code of conduct. Students also conduct research projects and they too should act ethically in their work. We should all genuinely wish to avoid harm to others, to avoid causing them any kind of distress, and respect their rights to freedom and privacy. Getting carried away with enthusiasm for a fascinating idea and clever research design can blind one to ethical pitfalls. Sensitivity is required together with a cool, objective appraisal of the proposed project. If in doubt you should seek the guidance and advice of your tutor or another professional.

The British Psychological Society's Ethical Principles for Conducting Research with Human Participants (1998) covers the principles described in Box 1.2. Section 2 of the Principles states:

'In all circumstances, investigators must consider the ethical implications and psychological consequences for the participants in their research. The essential principle is that the investigation should be considered from the standpoint of all participants: foreseeable threats to their psychological well-being, health, values or dignity should be eliminated. Investigators should recognise that, in our multi-cultural and multi-ethnic society and where investigations involve individuals of different ages, gender and social background, the investigators may not have sufficient knowledge of the implications of any investigation for the participants. It should be borne in mind that the best judge of whether an investigation will cause offence may be members of the population from which the participants in the research are to be drawn.'

---

**Box 1.2** *Items covered by the Ethical Principles for Conducting Research with Human Participants (British Psychological Society 1998)*

**Consent:** Participants must give willing and informed consent to participation in research studies.

**Deception:** Participants have the right not to be deceived during a study (though they often still are).

**Debriefing:** Participants should be told the true aim of studies after participation; questions about actual performance should be answered honestly; discussion should be used to monitor for possible negative effects or misconceptions.

**Withdrawal from an investigation:** Participants have the right to withdraw from the study at any time and should be reminded of

---

this by the researcher when situations become stressful and the participant might be inhibited from making a free decision to withdraw.

**Confidentiality:** All records of a participant's behaviour must be kept confidential. Anonymity must be guaranteed. Data are published by number or invented name.

**Protection of participants:** Participants must not be physically or psychologically harmed.

**Observational research:** Researchers should not observe people where they would not normally expect to be observed by strangers, or where cultural values conflict with the research.

**Giving advice (to participants):** Psychologists should offer advice when they become aware, through research procedures, of existing psychological or physical problems which might endanger the participant's future well-being.

**Monitoring of colleagues in the profession:** Psychologists should monitor the behaviour of fellow researchers with their participants.

## Conclusions

Experiments, once the mainstay of psychological research, now form only one type of approach used within psychological research, to gather evidence for theories. Increasing use is made of non-laboratory approaches and of qualitative methods, as some psychologists have become disillusioned with the narrowness and artificiality of a significant amount of experimentally based research. Psychologists can call on a wide variety of methods but all are used in the interests of keeping psychology a subject which relies on *empirical evidence* rather than on subjective, hunch, 'armchair' supposition or 'common sense'.

# Summary

- A **theory** is an attempted **explanation** of events in the world.
- In scientific investigation, theories are **supported** with publicly verifiable empirical data.
- Where variables are measured they must be **operationally defined**.
- **Support** does not imply **proof**; alternative explanations of events are always possible and the same data may support several of these alternative theories.
- In an attempt to retain theories, investigators attempt to rule out alternative explanations by gathering further data which eliminate the alternatives.
- Some contemporary research uses **qualitative methods** which involve gathering non-numerical data, mostly words and meanings. Proponents of these methods often argue that the hypothesis testing and mainly experimental approach described here tends to produce within modern psychology rather artificial and narrow theories and research.
- True experiments involve the manipulation of an **independent variable** and control of all other variables in order to identify a cause–effect relationship with a **dependent variable**.
- Other studies investigate differences between existing groups or correlations between existing variables.
- Questioning studies include the use of surveys, interviews and questionnaires.
- Semi-structured interviews gather qualitative data and can therefore be seen as producing more realistic and in-depth data; however, from another perspective they suffer from low reliability and difficulties of comparison; structured questionnaires and interviews make statistical comparison possible and relatively trustworthy. It is also possible to seek **replication** of such studies.

- Observation can be **qualitative** (often participant) or **quantitative** (often systematic or structured). If the latter, then observers must follow an agreed and tested coding scheme. In so-called **participant observation** the observer is in some way involved in the group under study and problems of replicability, reliability and subjectivity become more important issues.

- Case studies are in-depth investigations of one person or group, usually over a long period. They gather a great deal of qualitative and quantitative data to illuminate a particular, perhaps unique, condition or set of experiences.

- All researchers must follow a code of research ethics which concentrates on protection of the rights, comfort and safety of participants.

# EXPERIMENTAL AND NON-EXPERIMENTAL DESIGNS

**2**

## Introduction

This chapter introduces the reader to the precise meaning of an 'experiment' – an often misunderstood and misused term for research design. True experiments aim to demonstrate an unambiguous connection between cause and effect, but most research in psychology cannot achieve this aim. There are always several possible explanations for any effect shown. However, psychological researchers can try to eliminate as many alternative explanations as possible by operating a tight research procedure and by the accumulation of evidence from various types of research study.

## Experiments

Remember that the main feature of an experiment is the attempt to identify cause and effect by holding constant every variable except one (the independent variable) and observing any consequent change in the dependent variable. If such a relationship is demonstrated, psychologists tend to talk of finding an 'effect'. The main task in the *interpretation* of scientific experiments is to look carefully at what was done and how it was done (the design of an experiment) in order to see whether there are any other possible explanations of the effect found, other than that the independent variable caused the dependent variable to change. This is like saying 'It must be the food mixer that caused interference on the TV; when I switched it off the trouble stopped' and then thinking, 'but I wonder if there could be another cause; perhaps the plug or the socket or the circuit it is on or perhaps they just fixed the problem at the TV station when I turned the mixer off', and so on.

# Types of experimental design

## Independent samples design

In the last chapter we described an experiment in which there were two conditions with different participants in each. In *one* condition no litter was present and in the other, three crisp packets were on the floor. This type of experimental design is known as an *independent samples* design. Each person participates in only one condition of the experiment so their performance is *independent* of any performances in the other conditions. By contrast, in the *repeated measures* design described below, each person performs in all conditions of the experiment so their score in one condition is *related* to their score in the other conditions.

### Experimental conditions

In the littering study we used an *experimental condition*, that is, leaving three crisp packets on the floor. This condition contains the 'treatment' element of the independent variable. It is the factor that we introduce in order to observe its effects (if any) upon behaviour. It would be unwise to use only this condition since, if people did drop their litter, we would have no way of comparing with what they might do when there is *no* litter on the floor.

### Control conditions

The condition which provides a *baseline measure* of what people would do without the experimental treatment is known as a *control condition*.

A control condition occurs where participants experience everything that occurs in an experimental condition except for the 'treatment' of the independent variable.

### Control and experimental groups

In an independent samples design we have one group of participants experience the experimental condition while a separate group experience only the control condition. In this sort of design the groups are known as an *experimental group* and a *control group*.

### Placebo groups and conditions

Suppose that some clinical psychologists wish to compare the effects of a new type of therapy with the conventional style of counselling available in an institutional setting. The problem is that clients might improve with the new therapy because they think they should improve and not because of the particular features of the new approach. In such a design we might add a *placebo condition* where clients receive equivalent additional attention but not the new therapy itself. If attention *alone* is effective then both the experimental and placebo groups should improve over a control group, but if only the experimental group improves we can rule out any possible *placebo effect*. Physiological psychology experiments might use a placebo substance in one condition (e.g. salt) in order to rule out the possibility that participants' reactions to a tested chemical are merely psychological.

## Strengths and weaknesses of the independent samples design

### Participant variables

The independent samples design has one serious weakness. This is the comparability of the groups used. What if the people who are selected for the experimental condition just happen to be generally more untidy in their litter habits than the control group participants? This problem is a result of *participant variables*. With different people in each condition, it could be that differences between the groups on some crucial personality characteristic or ability are responsible for any difference found between group scores. *Our results may be confounded by differences between sample groups.*

There is a simple answer to this problem. We must *randomly allocate* participants to the two conditions. In this way we hope that roughly equal numbers of any such participant variable as untidiness will occur in each of the two conditions. Of course there will always be a *minor* discrepancy here but, with enough participants, this should have no serious effect on our results.

**Figure 2.1** *Participant variables may confound an experimental effect*

It also makes sense to assess, where possible, the participants' abilities before the experiment takes place, just to be sure that the two groups do not differ initially. For instance, if we are going to see whether a certain training method can improve memory for a word list, we could test each participant on a different, practice list, before commencing the proper experiment.

### The value of naïve participants

The strength of this design is that participants generally cannot know what is expected to happen. If we tested participants in *both* conditions of the litter study, they might well notice that in the second condition there are now several crisp packets on the floor and they may well guess what is expected to happen. They 'get wise' to the aims of the experiment.

Many experiments use a *vignette* approach. For instance, participants may be asked to read a scenario concerning a crime and to choose a sentence for the criminal. If the hypothesis is that males will receive harsher sentences than females, then one scenario will feature a female defendant while the other features a male defendant, with all other details (age, education, etc.) remaining the same. Obviously, participants given the scenario involving a male defendant would instantly guess the hypothesis if they were then given the female defendant scenario.

In addition to the advantage of keeping participants innocent of the research hypothesis, the independent samples design does not suffer with the other problems of *order effect* which we are about to encounter with the *repeated measures* design.

## Repeated measures designs

In many experiments we can use the same participants in both conditions; this is then a *repeated measures* design. For instance, we might ask participants to read a list of 20 names and then see how many they can recall when the list is removed. In a second condition we might ask them to read another list of names but this time with accompanying faces. Again we ask participants to recall as many as they can. We end up with pairs of *related* scores, a pair for each person, and this is why this design is one of a group known as *related designs*.

---

**PAUSE FOR THOUGHT**

If we are interested in whether faces aid recall, what would be the advantage of having participants complete *both* conditions?

---

In answer to the above we immediately avoid the problem encountered in the independent samples design of *participant variables* – that is, if people recall more names in the second condition this cannot be because these people just happen to be better at remembering names, since they are the *same* people. *Now* we are measuring each participant's recall performance in one condition against that *same* participant's performance in the second condition. In most cases this gives us a much more powerful design than that of independent samples. When it comes to statistical analysis we can simply say 'To what extent did *each person* improve?' rather than, 'Did one *group* do better than the other overall?' One group might do slightly better on average, but there may be wide variation *within* each group. In a repeated measures design we look at the difference between *each partici-pant's* performances.

## Strengths and weaknesses of the repeated measures design

We have just seen that a strength of the repeated measures design is that differences between conditions cannot be the result of dif-ferences between participant groups – participant variables are not a problem. A further advantage (though this is only a prac-tical point) is that the design is economical on participants, as each participant we can persuade into our experiment gives us two scores, one in each condition. To obtain equivalent data sets we need half the number of participants required in an indepen-dent samples design.

However, these advantages in design come at a certain cost in terms of the interpretation of any apparent experimental effect.

---

**PAUSE FOR THOUGHT**

In the name recall experiment, suppose participants did indeed recall more names in the second condition, which includes face pictures. Is this because of the pictures or could there be another reason for the improvement?

---

The participants may have improved simply because they have already had some practice at name recall (see Figure 2.2)

Where performance is affected by having performed the same task already, we talk of an *order effect*. Practice is not the only pos-sible order effect which might affect performance on the second recall task. Participants may get wise, or they may perform *worse* in the second condition because of *interference* from the first set of names they read. They may even perform worse because they are getting fed up with learning lists of names! Psychologists talk

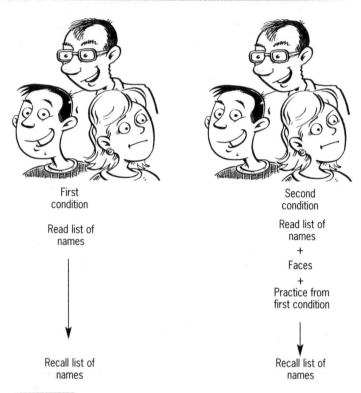

First
condition

Second
condition

Read list of
names

Read list of
names
+
Faces
+
Practice from
first condition

Recall list of
names

Recall list of
names

**Figure 2.2** *Faces* and *practice are present in the second condition of the name learning experiment*

of *fatigue* as a possible order effect which makes performance deteriorate in later conditions of an experiment.

### Counterbalancing – a solution to order effects

One traditional solution to the problem of order effects is to have half the participants perform the conditions of the experiment in one order (A then B), say no faces then faces, while the other half perform the conditions in the opposite order (B then A) – faces then no faces. This way the order effect does not disappear but its result should be spread evenly across the two conditions. Let's suppose people actually do much better in the faces condition. The participants in the AB order should improve on condition B because of the faces *and* because of practice, whereas the BA group will be better on condition B because of the faces but some of this difference will be lost because of their improvement through practice in condition A (which they undertake second).

### Randomisation – another solution to order effects

In many experiments there are several items in each condition of the independent variable. In our name recall experiment we are asking participants to read two lists of 20 names, one list in each condition. We could easily *merge* the two lists into one, so that for some names there would be a face picture and for some there would not. Similarly, where we investigate times to solve anagrams of both concrete and abstract words, we can present *both* conditions of the experiment simultaneously by mixing both types of anagram into one set (see Figure 2.3). The *order* of the items or trials is *randomised*, that is they are put into a random order. This way, on each trial, the participant does not get to expect one type or the other.

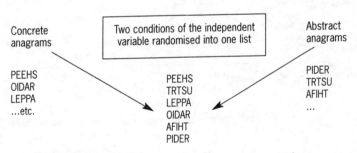

**Figure 2.3**    *Randomisation of stimulus materials or trials*

## Matched pairs design

On some occasions it is possible to get the best of both worlds in terms of repeated measures *and* independent samples designs. In an experiment where some children are to view an aggressive film and others a nature film (the control condition) in an attempt to assess the effects of aggressive films on subsequent aggressive behaviour, a researcher might *match* children on their initial aggressiveness. Then one of each of these pairs would be randomly allocated to the experimental condition while the other serves in the control condition. Again we end up with pairs of scores so this is another type of *related design*.

## Strengths and weaknesses of matched pairs designs

With matched pairs we avoid the problem of differing participant groups whilst retaining the advantage of repeated measures designs, in that we can treat our data in pairs and, for example, observe whether there is any difference between level of aggressiveness across each pair of children. Also, where a repeated measures design for a memory study would entail making two equivalent word lists for each participant to learn in the two conditions, here we can use the same list in each condition. A major problem however is that the matching may not be entirely effective or equal. In addition, if we lose one child from the study (say, because they move from the area) we can no longer make use of the results for the paired child.

**Table 2.1**    *Summary of strengths and weaknesses of common experimental designs*

| Experimental design | Strengths | Weaknesses |
|---|---|---|
| Independent samples | No order effects. Loss of one participant means loss of score from one condition only. | Variation between individuals in different groups (participant variables). Less economical on participants. |
| Repeated measures | No participant variables. More economical on participants. | Order effects. Loss of one participant means loss of a score from all conditions. |
| Matched pairs | No order effects. Minimal effect from participant variables. | Still some important difference between participants in different conditions is possible. |

## Laboratory and field studies

Let us return to the crisp packet study described in Chapter 1 and discussed earlier in this chapter. You might feel that this study is a little artificial and does not reflect everyday life (but see 'ecological validity', page 45, before deciding this). We certainly have the problem that participants in an experimental area of a university may behave far better than when on neutral territory. How might participants behave out on the street? Cialdini *et al.* (1990) provided an answer. These researchers handed leaflets to people who were about to walk down a particular path. Already lying in the path were 0, 1, 2, 4, 8 or 16 pieces of litter. This was the independent variable (with several levels). The dependent variable was whether or not the participant dropped the leaflet. Far more people dropped their leaflet in the conditions where more litter lay on the ground. We will talk about the results later on, but note for now that this is a *field study*. It has the distinct advantage of showing us how people, completely unaware of any psychological study, are apparently influenced by others' behaviour in an everyday situation.

In general the advantage of field studies, even when people know they are being investigated, is that they are studied in a familiar environment where behaviour is more likely to be similar to that which would occur without the investigation. You might like to contrast the observation of children's behaviour in a playroom at a university with their behaviour in their regular day nursery or when at home during the day. Of course, some field studies can be artificial too. For instance, children might be studied in their classroom but asked to complete quite unusual construction problems or written tests.

### *The point of artificiality in the laboratory*

There can be a 'knee-jerk' aspect to the reaction that laboratory studies in the human sciences simply *must* be artificial. One major aim of the laboratory has been *purposely* to make conditions artificial in order to control all variables and manipulate just one. The scientist does not always wish to generalise results *directly* from the laboratory to real life. Most often, a *theory* is tested in the laboratory, then, when that theory is *supported* by *experimental results*, researchers turn to looking at possible real-life applications. For instance, we can confirm the theory that all matter falls at the same rate by dropping a feather and a piece of coal in a jar under vacuum (quite unlike real life). Gas turbines and jet propulsion were studied quite separately in the laboratory before Frank Whittle had the idea of putting the two together to produce the first successful jet-engined human flight in 1941. Similarly, many psychologists would argue that we wish to extract specific behaviour from everyday life in order to study what would happen in the absence of other confounding variables which confuse the issue. Asch (1956) showed that extreme forms of conformity would increase *simply* with the addition of a few people agreeing with silly answers to simple questions.

### Problems with field studies

There are some disadvantages with field studies. First there is the ethical issue of *involuntary participation* (see Chapter 3). Second, there are problems with the interpretation of results because certain controls cannot be implemented. There may be variables which can alter beyond the researchers' control, such as weather conditions, presence of other pedestrians, noise and so on.

In the case of Cialdini's field research the most serious technical problem was that people could not be allocated to conditions at random. The researchers obviously had to take as 'participants' those who happened along the path set up for each condition. It could be that by chance more litter-prone people turned up for the condition using a high number of pieces of litter.

True experiments carried out in the field are known as *field experiments*. However, where the study is not an experiment we might refer to a *field investigation*. This term *includes* field experiments but also many other studies, such as Cialdini's, which we would refer to as a *quasi-experiment*.

# Quasi-experiments

The Cialdini study looks very much like an experiment. It has a clear independent variable (the varying amounts of litter on the ground) and this is controlled by the experimenter. However, we must remember that the original ideal of an experiment was to vary only one thing and to make *all* other conditions either the same or in some way controlled. The reason for this is that we can then claim quite logically that if there is significant change in the dependent variable this can *only* have been caused by variation in the independent variable. If we cannot allocate participants to conditions at random, then we cannot be sure that it is not a difference between the kinds of people in each condition that caused a difference in the dependent variable. The independent variable may not cause the differences found since the people themselves might differ.

When experiments carry this kind of ambiguity in their interpretation researchers often refer to them as 'quasi-experiments' – meaning 'very much like an experiment but lacking an important aspect of control'. In particular, quasi-experiments are said to occur where:

● participants are not randomly allocated to separate conditions (there are non-equivalent groups);
  and/or
● the experimenter does not control the independent variable.

## *Non-equivalent groups:*

This was the problem of non-random allocation to conditions, described above for Cialdini's study. Typical examples occur where applied psychologists, working (necessarily) in the field, have to use pre-existing groups for control and experimental conditions. A psychologist doing educational research, for example, may have to use one class in a school to test a new reading motivation programme, while another class acts as a control group.

### *Natural experiments:*

The second category of quasi-experiment includes those often termed *natural experiments*. Here an independent variable may occur naturally or at least in a real life situation beyond the researcher's control yet it is available for exploitation as a research subject. For instance, a psychologist might study differences in work attitudes in two branches of a company, one where a new incentive scheme has been introduced and one remaining on the old work conditions. Notice that here the researcher also has to contend with non-equivalent groups who might differ in average age, experience, income level, geographical area and so on. However, many statistical procedures are possible for accounting for these differences before claiming a difference in work attitude nevertheless exists between the two groups.

## Correlational and group difference studies

Many studies are not experiments at all. In Chapter 1 we said that it would be unethical to ask students to participate in an experiment where they had have five hours' sleep per night for a whole year. Instead we could use existing data. Non-experimental studies using information that already exists are often referred to as *ex post facto* studies (after the fact). For instance, we can look at the relationship between the average number of hours' sleep each student had per night through the year and their exam grade. Such a relationship (shown in Figure 5.4, page 130) is known as a *correlation* between pairs of values (see page 129). If our theory is correct we would expect exam grades to be higher as we look at people with more hours' sleep per night.

Such studies are sometimes known as 'correlational' because we would use a statistical correlation to assess the relationship between sleep and exam grade values. However, we might instead identify two samples of students (as suggested in Chapter 1), one group who have had an average of five or fewer hours' sleep per night and another with an average of eight hours' or more sleep. Statistically speaking we would now look at a *difference* between these two groups on exam grade, rather than a correlation, but the study would nevertheless be non-experimental.

Why do we call these studies non-experimental? Well, we must ask whether anything in the design helps us to establish what is cause and what is effect. In this case there is nothing. A correlation or group difference would support the idea that more sleep leads to better exam grades. However, it is also just as possible that 'better sleep' is a *result* of higher exam grades. People who are successful in exams may decide on better sleep in order to continue with their educational success. More likely, both better sleep *and* better grades may be a function of a generally more studious approach to life. For most correlational results there are usually these three possible cause–effect directions to explain the relationship between the two variables (see Figure on page 140).

## Using a pre-test

We can often turn what would otherwise be correlational studies into quasi-experiments using a *pre-test*. Suppose we argue that better sleep leads to better study motivation (which in turn leads to better revision). We measure study motivation using some form of paper and pencil test questionnaire like those described in Chapter 3. We can measure students' levels of study motivation at the start of the academic year. At the end of their course we identify groups who had 'good' and 'bad' sleep patterns over the year. If we find that these groups did not differ in study motivation at the start of their course, but that they do now, we have stronger (but not watertight) evidence that 'better' sleep was a factor in *creating* higher levels of study motivation.

Similarly we can assess groups of males and females before starting their careers in, say, a large computer corporation. If the groups are equivalent on education level, motivation, abilities and other relevant variables, including attendance records, yet females do not progress as well as the males, we have strong support for the claim that lack of promotion is associated with being female.

## Group difference studies

In the example above, if we simply enter the organisation and select two samples, one of males, one of females, finding that the female group is further behind on promotion, we have no way of knowing whether the two groups started out as equivalent. If we find that extroverts differ from introverts on self-confidence we have no idea which variable caused what effect. This is because extroversion and gender are not 'treatments'. In a true or quasi-experiment there is a treatment given in one condition, which does not occur in another. Extroversion is not 'applied' to anyone at any specific time nor is one's gender, except in the extreme sense of all through one's life. Most studies of group differences are so lacking in the controls that help isolate cause and effect that they do not even qualify for description as quasi-experiments.

Such group difference studies give us no more information than do correlational studies; they are really a version of the same sort of study. We can *correlate* extroversion scores with self-confidence scores or we can look at the *difference* in self-confidence between those with high and low extroversion scores. We get the same sort of information in either case.

## Cross-sectional and longitudinal studies
### Cross-sectional studies

A special kind of group difference study occurs where researchers select a cross-section (e.g. of ages or educational levels), to explore for instance a theory about stages of child development. To test Kohlberg's theory of stages of moral reasoning, samples of 10-, 13- and 16-year-old children might be selected in order to demonstrate different kinds of reasoning at different ages. Of course, in such a study it is essential to cancel out all other possible confounding variables by making the samples as similar as possible on other variables, such as socio-economic status and level of education.

### Longitudinal studies

We can avoid the problems of finding equivalent samples by using another, much slower way to assess moral reasoning at different ages. In a longitudinal study we follow the *same* group of children across the age range just mentioned. The main problem here is the length of the study and the possible loss of participants from the study before the final stage has been reached.

# Validity in experiments

When we run an experiment we want to be able to conclude that our particular independent variable did indeed cause any difference found in the dependent variable. We want to argue that the independent variable is responsible for the *effect*. If something else in fact caused the effect, and we assume our independent variable was the cause, we would be drawing an *invalid* conclusion. In the name recall experiment described earlier, for instance, it could be *practice* at learning lists of names that causes improvement in the second condition. If the second condition were always the 'names plus faces' condition then it would be *invalid* to conclude that the faces were responsible for the effect found (the recorded improvement in recall – see Figure 2.2). Nor would it be valid to conclude that the independent variable affected the dependent variable if the difference in performance we obtained was a result of 'chance alone' or was only an apparent difference, caused by the inappropriate use of statistics.

| A **valid** conclusion | independent variable ⟶ change in dependent variable |
|---|---|
| An **invalid** conclusion | independent variable + confounding variable ⟶ change in dependent variable |
| An **invalid** conclusion | no *real* change in dependent variable; apparent differences were caused by sampling error (see p.53) or inappropriate use of statistical analysis (see Chapter 5). |

Researchers talk of the *validity* of experimental findings. They also see possible alternative explanations as 'threats to validity'. These alternative explanations can often be avoided if the *design* of the study is carefully thought out beforehand.

Here is an outline of a study in which the researcher has found a significant effect – the independent variable appears to have affected the dependent variable.

---

**PAUSE FOR THOUGHT**

Two teachers decide to try out a new mathematics teaching method to see whether it increases pupils' understanding of their maths enough to affect end of term grades. One teacher continues with the existing method in her class, while the other uses the new method which involves the purchase of new books and the use of computers. At the end of three months the pupils are tested and the experimental group do much better. The teachers assume that the new method is responsible for the improvement of one group over the other.

What factors might be responsible for the difference here other than the new teaching method used? That is, what threats to the validity of the teachers' conclusion are there?

---

There are many possible alternative explanations here but the most obvious weaknesses in this design are:

- There are different teachers in each condition – difference may be caused solely by teachers' styles.
- There are different pupils in each condition – pupils might already be different in ability.
- The new method involves new books and computers – either of these factors and not the new method itself – might be responsible for the improvements.
- Pupils know they are subject to the new method – this knowledge alone might make them work harder and learn better.
- Teachers know what should happen – they may influence the results.

## Internal or construct validity

Any feature of a research design which could result in an invalid conclusion about the real nature of an effect can be termed a threat to *internal validity* or *construct validity*. These are not the same thing although there is some overlap (see Coolican, 1999). They generally refer to factors which might *confound* or factors, like bad sampling or statistical errors, which lead us to conclude that X causes Y when in fact it does not. It is these sorts of problem with the interpretation of an experimental effect that we shall investigate further in Chapter 3.

## External validity

Where an effect is genuine (that is, it *is* caused by the manipulation of an independent variable) – we can ask how far we can generalise this effect. This special type of validity of findings is known as *external validity*.

There are several ways in which we might be able or unable to generalise any effect beyond the specific situation in which it was demonstrated. Researchers are concerned with:

- validity across *settings – ecological validity*;
- validity across *people – population validity*;
- validity over *time –* e.g. does the effect work now like it did in the 1960s?

### *Ecological validity*

*Ecological validity* refers to the problem of being able to generalise an effect from the particular setting in which it is demonstrated. As stated above, 'failure' in an experimental laboratory might not generalise to 'failure' in ordinary tasks, when no scientific experiment is involved. This would be an example of a problem with ecological validity. Very often we say that an effect shown in a laboratory may not be one which would occur in a natural setting, where many other variables influence behaviour. In a famous series of experiments, Asch (1956) showed that one student would quite often agree with a very silly answer to a question if six other apparently naïve students had already given the same silly answer. The students were in fact confederates who had previously agreed with the experimenter that they would give silly answers to set questions. In real life, if we found our ourselves completely opposed to all members of a group because of a view we hold, we might seek support from friends, read up on supportive literature, keep our view to ourselves and so on. The Asch situation is quite unlike real life – it lacks *mundane realism*. There again, the value of Asch's conformity experiments was exactly that they showed, when all other variables are removed in a laboratory setting, just how far people will conform to ridiculous opinions.

Milgram's classic obedience findings were generalised to many different settings, including a seedy downtown office, demonstrating that it was not just the prestige of Yale University that caused people to obey commands to carry on hurting a victim. Hofling *et al.* (1966) conducted a well-known experiment in which nurses were asked by an unknown doctor, by telephone, to administer larger than maximum doses of an unfamiliar medicine. This broke several of the hospitals' rules but, nevertheless, 21 out of 22 nurses obeyed. However, a replication of this study failed to find any such effect. Milgram's study can be said to possess ecological validity whereas the findings of Hofling's study appear limited to the setting in which the research was carried out (perhaps that particular hospital at that particular time under that particular management regime.)

Hofling's study is more naturalistic in its setting but an attempt to generalise the findings failed and this therefore fails to provide ecological validity for the apparent effect.

### Population validity

Very many psychological research studies have been carried out on students, very often psychology students (Sears, 1986). This is because these people are usually the most convenient for researchers in universities to test. However, in many topic areas the fact that the participants are students might make quite a big difference to what is shown. In a study on conformity to political attitudes, students will not represent as broad a range as would a sample from the general public. Research findings may then be limited to populations similar to the students rather than society in general.

Smith & Bond (1997) demonstrate that the vast majority of studies cited in one US and one UK social psychology textbook are studies from the USA. Two-thirds of the studies in the UK textbook are from the USA, almost one-third from Europe, but only 2 per cent come from the rest of the world with just 1.2 per cent of these from the Australasian area. The US textbook contains just 2 per cent from Europe and slightly more than this from the rest of the world.

Clearly there would be something wrong with concluding from many of these social psychology studies that '*People* tend to ....'. We should say something more like 'Students in the USA tend to …' or 'White people in the UK tend to …', until we know that the effect has *population validity* by trying the study design out on samples from different populations.

### Cross-cultural studies

*Cross-cultural studies* are another type of *group difference* study in which a psychological effect found in one culture (usually Western) is tested in another culture, to see whether the effect is relatively *universal*, that is, common across cultures. Several effects have been found to reverse in cultures that are more *collectivist* (an emphasis on co-operative economies and traditional family ties and roles) than they are *individualistic* (typical of 'Western cultures' with an emphasis on individual achievement). For instance, the *self-serving bias*, reported in Western textbooks, finds individuals attributing their successes to personal abilities and their failures to external circumstances, for example 'I passed because of my skill; I failed because the test was too difficult'. In Japan and other more collectivist societies the reverse of this tends to occur, with people saying they are lucky when they win and criticising their efforts when they fail.

## Conclusions

Experiments can lead to very precise discoveries about the relationships between variables. However, the design of each experiment must be carefully thought out so that as many possible alternative explanations and confounding variables as possible are ruled out. Experiments in the field may lead to less artificiality, but they tend to introduce more problematic extraneous and potentially confounding variables. Studies with no manipulation of an independent variable at all, such as correlations and group difference studies, produce an even greater number of ambiguous interpretations. The study of experimental validity should lead us to analyse carefully the possible sources of weakness in our designs and help us to create better research studies in the future.

The essence of research design is the avoidance of as many kinds of *threats to the validity* of our studies as possible. The next chapter deals with various possible biases that can occur in research designs and procedures, and ways in which they might be avoided.

## Summary

- The **independent samples** experimental design involves different people in each condition of an experiment. A problem arises as a result of the very differences between people which may form the alternative explanation of why an effect did or did not 'work'.
- The **repeated measures** design (a type of related design) solves this by having each person participate in all conditions of the experiment. However, this introduces the possible confounding variable of an **order effect** which can be partially

dealt with using **counterbalancing** or, better, **randomisation** of the stimuli presented in the different conditions of the independent variable.

- In a **matched pairs** design a participant in one condition of an experiment is paired with a member of the other condition on a relevant basis such as educational level, age and so on.
- **Laboratory studies** are better able to control variables but might be criticised for some artificiality compared with **field experiments** or **field studies** in general, where participants behave in an everyday context.
- **Quasi-experiments** are said to occur where either the researcher cannot allocate participants at random to conditions, or the researcher does not manipulate the independent variable, as in a **natural experiment**.
- In **correlational** and **group difference** studies there is usually no control at all over an independent variable and the grouping variable (e.g. gender or introversion/extroversion) does not involve any kind of experimental 'treatment' of a group compared with a control group. Such studies may throw up differences to support theories but, without certain other careful measures and checks, are exceedingly ambiguous to interpret and are not really 'experimental' in nature at all.
- **Cross-sectional studies** use samples from different categories of a population dimension (age, class etc.) to make a current comparison between these categories.
- In a **longitudinal study** the comparison is made on the same group as time passes.
- **Validity** in experiments refers to the confidence with which we can be sure we have identified a true cause–effect relationship.
- **Threats to validity** are design features which permit an alternative explanation of the effect. Threats to **internal validity** and **construct validity** refer to variables which might be responsible for the apparent effect other than the independent variable.

- Threats to **external validity** concern the extent to which we may safely generalise the effect to other settings, populations and times.
- **Cross-cultural studies** compare groups from different cultures on a psychological variable or effect.

# CONTROLS AND BIASES IN A VARIETY OF RESEARCH SETTINGS

**3**

## Introduction

In this chapter we look at a variety of possible threats, from people, settings and measures to the validity of research findings and the ways in which some of these can be avoided. First we look at the *selection* of people for research studies and the ways in which bias at this stage can lead to problems in the interpretation of results. We then look at the *research setting* and the ways in which the *social interaction* between researchers and those they research can lead to distortions in what is studied and recorded. Next, we look at the *standardisation of procedures* which should lead to a minimum amount of variation, through random errors, in the testing stages of a research project. Finally we examine the *measures* used by researchers and ways in which these need to be reliable and valid.

## Who shall we study? – sampling issues and populations

### The need for representative samples

When greengrocers lay out their vegetables they tend to put their best fruits on top. What you see is not *representative* of the fruit you are likely to get if you purchase some. Sensibly, what you do is to *sample* the fruit underneath to get a better idea of what the goods are like *in general*. In psychological research we use samples of *people* in order to test our theories. These too need to be representative if we are to generalise our findings from a few people to the population from which they were selected.

## Samples are always from populations

Notice here that a *population* refers to all the individuals in a category, be they people or tomatoes. When we talk of a population we tend to think of the population of a country or town, but in psychology (and statistics generally) a population can be a rather abstract or infinite notion. For instance, the population of scores that we could gather in a memory task is infinite because we could test the same people many times over. Scores on a spelling test for the population of 12-year-olds in the UK would be virtually impossible to gather, not least because some would become 13 by the time we could get round to test them all! Hence, statisticians have developed sophisticated techniques for *estimating* measures for a whole population by taking *samples*, that is, smaller selections from a population. This is rather like the way in which we might sample fruit for size if we were buying in bulk. The techniques used by statisticians are however, far more sophisticated and precise, although the reasoning is the same. In order to make accurate estimates of populations the samples used *must* be *representative* of the populations they are drawn from. We must be able to say that if this *sample* has certain properties, the whole population is probably like that too. When researchers set out to sample people for study they need to have in mind what is their *sampling frame* – this will be the target population from which their samples will be drawn.

---

**PAUSE FOR THOUGHT**

Suppose you had to find out students' opinions about proposed new library opening arrangements. How would you propose to find the views of a *representative* sample of students in order to report back the *general* view of students to the college authorities?

---

You could:

● stand outside the library and ask those who are willing to talk to you;

- visit classes in the most popular subjects and distribute questionnaires;
- leave a comments box in the entrance hall;
- enlist a team to chat to everyone they possibly can in the student refectory.

## Biased samples and sampling error

All these methods would probably highlight important views held by many students in the school or college. However, each method would also fail to test certain types of student from what could be very important categories. Where samples exclude certain types or categories of people, or where they *over-represent* other types or categories, they are said to be *biased samples*. To the extent that the sample characteristics differ from the population characteristics we are said to have made a *sampling error*. If, for instance, 60 per cent of our sample are opposed to the new regulations and we assume that therefore 60 per cent of the student population are similarly opposed, we would be making quite a serious sampling error if only 25 per cent of all students are *in fact* opposed.

---

**PAUSE FOR THOUGHT**

In each of the examples just given, and in your own proposed sampling method, think of all the types or categories of people who would not be included in the samples taken.

---

To take the above bullet points in the same order:

- you would miss people unwilling to talk and people who do not use the library;
- you would miss those in less popular subjects and those who skip classes;
- only observant, conscientious writers who use the entrance hall would respond;
- only those using the refectory and those liked by the team members might be included.

## Obtaining a representative sample – probability based samples

### Random samples

In popular thinking a 'random sample' is just a haphazard one, but in technical terms the definition is much more precise. Let us examine the definition and then think about why the examples above come nowhere near it.

**In a simple random sample every member of the sampling frame has an equal chance of being selected.**

Another way of saying this is that all sampling bias has been eliminated. There are other ways to satisfy this definition but in a *simple random sample* every combination of people selected is equally likely. If we take several large enough random samples they will form a very good representation of the population they were taken from.

We can see that the methods of sampling students described above in no way produce this complete lack of sampling bias. Each method would systematically omit certain categories of people and focus more strongly on other categories.

### How to sample randomly

There are three main ways to draw a simple random sample:

**Computer selection:** with many types of software we can get the computer to select a random sample from a larger set of data.

**Random number tables:** a non-electronic method is to use tables of random numbers. Starting anywhere in Table 8, Appendix 2, moving vertically or horizontally, a random sequence of numbers is produced. Five people can be selected at random from a group of 50, by giving each person in the group a number from 1 to 50 and selecting those who hold the first five numbers which occur as you move through the table.

**Lottery method:** you can select a sample of 30 from the college population by simply giving *every* student a number and drawing 30 numbers from a well shuffled barrel, lottery style.

## Stratified samples

Although repeated small, random samples will eventually give a representative picture of the population, we often cannot trust chance to deliver a representative sample on one specific occasion. What we can do instead is to ensure that important sections of the population *are* proportionately represented in our sample. Suppose we know that 10 per cent of students study A levels, 26 per cent GCSE subjects, 35 per cent take NVQ-related courses and so on. We can sample from each of these strata by ensuring that proportions of the relevant strata within the population are reflected in the same proportions within the sample. Here, 10 per cent of our sample would be A level students, 26 per cent GCSE and so on. To get the 10 per cent of A level students, however, we would need to sample randomly from among all A level students, and we would obtain 26 per cent of our sample by sampling randomly among all GCSE students, and so on.

## Systematic sampling

A near-random method of selecting participants is to take every *n*th person in a list. If we want to select 20 students from 200 to interview we might take the alphabetic register of 200 names and select every tenth name. This method is known as *systematic sampling* or *quasi-random sampling*. It is improved by making the starting point on the list a random choice. We randomly select a number from one to 20, say 17, then take the seventeenth person, the twenty-seventh, the thirty-seventh and so on, again giving everybody an equal chance of being selected.

# Non-probability based samples

It is not always possible to obtain absolutely representative samples. Certainly, a simple random sample drawn from a large population is an extreme rarity in psychological research. Indeed, many samples consist of those participants the researchers are lucky enough to be able to 'recruit' at the time of the project. To the extent that samples are not representative there are greater threats to *population validity*. In such a case we must be quite wary in generalising any results to the wider population of people.

## Self-selecting samples

In many psychological studies no real attempt at random selection is made. Large scale representative sampling tends to occur mainly in survey and interview work. Psychological experiments often rely for their sample on those who will volunteer or, in North American universities at least, those who choose this particular study for their obligatory participation (students in the USA are often required to participate in at least one study but they may choose which one). Such volunteers are *self-selecting*, as are those who answer media advertisements requesting participants. For instance, field studies may use a noticeboard to recruit mothers and children attending a health centre.

## Opportunity samples

This term is a favourite in the writing-up of psychology practical reports. It means no more than that the participants used were conveniently available at the time (typically the class of students itself) and may also be called a *convenience sample*.

## Snowball samples

In qualitative work interviewers often do not require a random sample at all, nor even a fully representative one. What might be required are key people who can report on the feelings of a community or who can help with trying to understand a particular phenomenon under research, such as reasons for street gang fighting. Here, key individuals are found from initial interviews. One person's interview can produce a 'snowball' effect as each new lead turns into several more leads.

# People investigating people – researcher effects and participant reactivity

## Researchers and experimenters

We said in Chapter 1 that there was a fundamental difference between psychology and most other sciences in that psychologists investigate other people. Psychological researchers, just like anybody else, cannot help but have certain expectations about how others will behave. Even expectations about how experimental rats will behave seem to be a factor to consider in psychological research. Rosenthal & Lawson (1964) showed that when students were told that their rats were 'Skinner-box bright', they ended up with faster learning rats than students who had been told that their rats were 'Skinner-box dull'. The only problem was that the rats had actually been randomly allocated to the students! In a classic study by Rosenthal & Jacobson (1968), when it was arranged for teachers to 'overhear' that certain children in their class should make late gains in their academic development, these same children actually *did* make the expected progress. Eden (1990) demonstrated the same sort of effect when army leaders were told (incorrectly) that their platoon members were above average.

These studies suggest that when researchers have clear *expectations* about what should happen in their research study, this can have an effect on the outcome. In other words, to some extent, researchers find what they are expecting to find, simply because they are expecting to find it! There are many more studies, reported in Rosnow & Rosenthal (1997), which support this possibility*. It is not that researchers knowingly influence their results in a certain direction. Fortunately, cases of known

---

*Rosnow and Rosenthal's text is highly recommended for its very interesting coverage of many aspects of biasing effects, confounding variables, interpersonal effects, characteristics of volunteer participants and several ethical issues in experimental research.

deliberate falsification are rare in scientific history and in psychological research. The effects of researcher expectancy are subtle and probably not the result of conscious 'fiddling' of the procedure. However, as we shall see, researchers can employ controls in their designs that help eliminate the possibility that their knowledge of expected results has 'helped' the results to fall the way that they have.

## Controlling for researcher expectations
### Blind procedures

A *blind procedure* is one in which the people who run an experiment, and/or take measures of the dependent variable, are not aware of the expected research outcomes (i.e. the hypotheses being tested or the value of the independent variable). This way the assessors' expectancies cannot influence results. The measures might include coding behaviour or rating interview content. This way, although no one actually distrusts the assistants, the validity of the research project is not weakened by the possibility of bias from knowing research staff. Well, not too much at least. It may still be possible for researchers to detect the condition or group that participants are in and either unwittingly bias results towards the hypothesis or overcompensate in trying not to. Rosenthal *et al.* (1965) showed that participants higher in need for social approval tended to turn up earlier at the experimental site. Rosnow & Rosenthal (1997) argue that experimenters may therefore easily 'spot' which participants belong to the 'highly anxious' group.

## Observer/rater reliability

The codes that assistants record when observing behaviour can be checked for *reliability*. In this context *observer reliability* means that the *same* pieces of behaviour are coded in the *same* way by *different observers*. This would also apply where, for instance, research assistants have to listen to interview recordings and rate the content for, say, 'warmth' shown by fathers towards their children or anxiety shown by interviewees in discussing their feelings about computers. Again, we would expect different raters to give the same or very similar ratings to the same interview content. Where reliability turns out to be rather poor we might have to start the coding over again, re-train observers/raters or even abandon the data gathered and start anew.

## Participants

Participants too might influence results by knowing what is expected of them. That participants do develop expectations which influence recorded behaviour was shown dramatically by Orne & Scheibe (1964). They showed that participants reacted to 'deprivation' (five hours alone in a room) in a more extreme manner if they had first been shown a 'panic button' and asked to sign a consent form. Orne (1962) coined the term *'demand characteristics'* to refer to the ways in which participants try to appraise a research situation and guess what is expected of them. Orne stated:

'The totality of cues that convey an experimental hypothesis to the subject become significant determinants of the subject's behaviour. We have labelled the sum total of such cues as the 'demand characteristics of the experimental situation' (Orne, 1962, page 779).

## Participant reactivity

Participants in experiments are not like the inert bits of matter that physicists work on. Participants are people and they interact with research staff as they do generally with other people in social situations. Particularly when situations are unfamiliar, we need to constantly interpret what is going on, what will happen next, what are other people's motives and what we are expected to do. Participants may react to any changing variables they perceive in the research situation, not just those that the researcher manipulates. People may react simply to the fact they are under observation. This was demonstrated many years ago in the famous Hawthorne studies conducted in the late 1920s and the 1930s (Roethlisberger & Dickson, 1939). Here, one surprising finding was that workers appeared to alter their behaviour towards greater productivity no matter in what direction the environmental stimuli were altered. For instance, productivity increased when overhead lighting intensity was increased or when it was decreased. Sensitivity to the fact of being observed or tested is known as *participant reactivity*. A particularly important aspect of this is *evaluation apprehension* – the anxiety participants experience at having their behaviour evaluated in a research situation. People may attempt to be 'good' research participants by 'pleasing the experimenter'. Some participants in Asch's studies, described in Chapter 2, said, when interviewed afterwards, that they did not wish to mess up Asch's results so, despite their private judgements, they had gone along with the majority view of the group.

## Social desirability

Participants may wish to please the experimenter in order not to 'spoil' the results, or they may wish to maintain a publicly acceptable image. By *social desirability* we mean that participants may wish to 'look good'. Parents interviewed about their methods of child discipline are hardly likely to bare their soul about their worst lapses, especially when they are well aware that techniques such as spanking are widely disapproved of. People who guess that a study is about prejudice may keep unacceptable attitudes to themselves.

## Controlling for participant expectation and reactivity effects

### Single and double blind procedures

In very many research studies, participants are unaware of the research hypotheses, or they are deliberately misled. They may be told that the experiment is only about the overt task they are set to perform and not about the true independent variable. In Latané & Darley's (1968) studies, for instance, participants were asked to engage in a task such as filling in a form or having a discussion when, in fact, the experiment concerned the participants' helping reactions when 'an emergency' occurred. These designs, of course, incur the ethical issue of deception, mentioned in Chapter 1.

In the case of Latané & Darley's studies, participants could be said to be *blind* to the overall purpose of the experimental conditions. However, in some studies participants may be aware of the research aims and of the purpose of two different conditions. However, they can be kept unaware of which condition they are actually in. Such a procedure would be described as using a *single blind* design. Where experimenters too are unaware of the participant's condition (as described earlier) this is a *double blind* design. For instance, neither participant nor experimental assistant may know whether the participant has swallowed an active chemical or a *placebo* substance (see page 30).

### *Unwitting or involuntary participation*

An obvious way to avoid all participant expectancy effects is to conduct studies in which participants are completely unaware that they are being studied. This again raises serious ethical issues. Cialdini *et al.*'s (1990) study, described in Chapter 2, involved giving members of the public a leaflet and observing whether they dropped it or not. The intervention in people's lives here seems minimal – people are given leaflets in the street all the time – so the ethical issue appears none too pressing. Observation of people in shopping malls should present no problems, as the behaviour is public anyway and no intervention occurs. However, in studies like that of Piliavin, Rodin & Piliavin (1969), where people went to the aid of an apparently sick actor, and in several participant observation studies, such as Rosenhan's study of staff in psychiatric institutions, unwitting involvement is a very serious consideration against carrying out the research project. In some participant observation studies, people give in depth, private and intimate details, or have notes taken on their private behaviour, all without their knowledge of any research project occurring. Humphreys (1970) recorded intimate details of homosexual behaviour in a public lavatory, even taking car registration numbers in order to interview people later on, all in a covert manner – he took the role of a 'lookout' checking for the arrival of police. Here, several principles of psychologists' contemporary code of ethical behaviour are contravened.

Student researchers should always check with a tutor if they are contemplating any form of covert data recording or intervention where those observed will be unwitting participants in the research project.

### Controlling for social desirability

The best way to avoid social desirability effects would *also* be to use a design in which participants are completely unaware of being observed, if one could avoid any negative ethical implications. Otherwise, to avoid the possibility that participants will behave or perform in accordance with what they think will 'look good', they can, of course, be warned that true, rather than ideal, reports and events are required to make a useful research contribution.

Some questionnaires (see page 65) include a 'lie scale'. This involves items that would only be agreed with by a person of extremely high moral and social standards (e.g. 'I have never been late for any appointment'; 'I have never lost my temper'). Results from participants answering in too 'good' a manner are not used in the final analysis. This does not mean that participants are assumed to be lying, just that, in order to be sure that one is not including respondents who are trying to 'look good', we exclude any who score above a certain criterion score in the 'good' direction. This may of course mean that perfectly good and very moral respondents are excluded from the final analysis in the interests of research validity.

A cunning technique, but one which has attracted a fair amount of criticism on ethical grounds, is that of the 'bogus pipeline', introduced by Jones & Sigall (1971). Here, a participant is led to believe that the experimenter's equipment is capable of detecting any untruths they may produce. This is achieved by securing information about the participant that they have not yet knowingly disclosed to the experimenter (such as their place of birth or mother's name). When the participant is asked to lie to some of these items the experimenter is able to demonstrate that the equipment 'detects their lie' and, apparently, participants given this experience are more open and forthcoming on sensitive issues. However, it is unlikely that this equipment would pass current ethical criteria for research, certainly in the UK.

# Standardised procedures – controlling extraneous variables

One very general way of attempting to reduce bias that can enter the research procedure through participant and experimenter expectancies, is to ensure that the testing procedure is exactly the same for all participants. Such a *standardised procedure* involves giving experimenters exact instructions on how to proceed with each participant. If all participants are treated in exactly the same way this should, in theory, reduce the possibility for *extraneous variables* to influence proceedings (such as giving some participants more help or attention than others).

### Extraneous variables

Extraneous variables (sometimes called *situational variables*) are any that threaten to produce inconsistency in our measures of behaviour (such as temperature changes, noise levels, superfluous speech from the experimenter and so on). Although we try to control all other variables in an experiment which might have some unwanted effect on behaviour, it is interesting to note just how far humans can maintain behaviour in the face of extreme distraction. Hovey (1928) asked two groups of students to complete an intelligence test, one in a quiet room and the other in a room where there were 'seven bells, five buzzers, a 550 watt spotlight, a 90,000 volt rotary spark gap, a phonograph, two organ pipes of varying pitch, three metal whistles, a 55 pound circular saw, a photographer taking pictures and four students doing acrobatics!'. There was, apparently, no difference in the performance of the two groups!

Interpersonal variables are perhaps more powerful and more potentially distracting. With a rigidly standardised procedure it should not matter whether, for instance, participant or experimenter are male or female, quiet or talkative, questioning or passive. However, that interactions between opposite sexes can be influential was shown by Rosenthal (1966). Male experimenters smiled at only 12 per cent of their male participants but 70 per cent of their female participants. They were also more likely to use a female participant's name and to look directly at her. Apparently both males and females take longer to gather data from a participant of the opposite sex than a same-sex participant (Rosnow & Rosenthal, 1997).

Standardised procedures then, even if they are hard to follow exactly for every experimenter with every participant, should make some difference in terms of reducing the number and variety of biases that can enter into data collection. Many experiments are run on computers these days, especially in the area of cognitive psychology, and the advantage here is that, apart from initial instructions, there is a minimum of human interaction. The computer programme really shouldn't be able to influence behaviour or be influenced by characteristics of the participants.

# Questionnaires and testing materials

Psychologists have developed an enormous array of questionnaires and tests used in an attempt to measure psychological characteristics or human abilities. Although not all researchers subscribe to the complete testing theory, the general assumptions of this theory are that:

- human characteristics can be measured;
- measures developed are instruments like any other measurement tool and are subject to error;
- errors come from either faults in the measuring instrument or random errors associated with the testing situation (such as noise or distraction);
- tests need to be *standardised* on the population to be sampled;
- tests need to be *reliable* and *valid*.

## Reliability, validity and standardisation of tests and scales

### Standardisation of tests and measures

Any measure needs to be standardised. It is no use you telling me that you have given me the kilo of tomatoes I paid for and then informing me that you are using your own measurement system where a kilo is equal to 500 'old' grams. A *standardised* psychological test is one that has been tried out on large samples of a specific population (say, UK eight-year-olds) so that any single member of the population can be measured and compared with the overall population. We cannot measure *all* UK eight-year-olds, but we can *estimate*, using powerful statistical techniques, the *norms* for that population. Norms are standards, for example that 50 per cent of UK eight-year-olds score more than 40 on a particular reading test. Note here that the standardisation of tests is a different matter from the standardisation of experimental *procedures* discussed above. They share the same name but are different in emphasis.

## Reliability of tests and measures

If a test is *reliable* then it is *consistent* – it measures the same thing at the same value on separate occasions, no matter who uses it, just as a weighing machine should. For psychological tests there is a simple method for assessing reliability. Using for instance, an anxiety scale, *test–retest reliability* would involve testing a group of participants on the scale then testing the same group again six months later. The two sets of scores are then *correlated* (see page 129). A strong correlation indicates a reliable measure.

### Inter-observer or inter-rater reliability

As was described earlier, assessment of the reliability of various observers and raters (for example of interview content) can also be achieved using correlation of the sets of scores with one another. For instance, Observer A's scores for child 1, child 2, child 3, etc. should be fairly similar to Observer B's scores for these same children.

## Validity of tests and measures

If measures are *valid* then they really do measure the variable they are intended to measure. It would be unhelpful if a weighing machine actually measured, or significantly responded to, the local temperature. An anxiety test should measure just that and *not* people's self-confidence instead (though the two may well be *related*). Tests of validity are made by various means. A common method is to employ some form of *criterion validity*. If a test is a measure of current anxiety state then we should certainly find changes if a group has just been subjected to a frightening experience. With this in mind researchers might take anxiety measurements for a group of smokers before and after a film about the serious health hazards of smoking.

## What do psychological tests and scales measure?

Table 3.1 shows that there are a variety of types of test measuring different kinds of human characteristic. A major division is between 'best performance' tests and 'typical performance' tests. When assessing ability to do verbal problems, aptitude for computer programming or knowledge of psychology, we really want to know what is pretty well the *best* you can do. When assessing a subject's usual state of anxiety, self-confidence, aggression or attitude on genetic modification of foods, we usually want to know their *typical* behaviour or state. A few tests do attempt to discriminate between the subject's state *now* and the more *typical* trait of, for example, anxiety.

**Table 3.1**    *Types of psychological test*

| Type of test | Aim of test | Type of behaviour/ response | Example |
|---|---|---|---|
| Ability | what you are able to do (skill rather than knowledge) | best | reading test |
| Aptitude | what you can become capable of; your potential ability | best | programming, training selection |
| Attainment | what you have achieved (often knowledge rather than skill) | best | psychology examination |
| Personality | what you are typically *like* | typical | extroversion |
| States | how you are *now* | actual | current anxiety |
| Attitude | what you think about an issue; your beliefs or at least your public response to the issue | typical | views on free immigration |

Attitude scales are very popular in student psychology projects but there are many points to consider in their construction. For a fairly detailed account, especially on the types of items to be used and several major pitfalls in their wording, see Coolican (1999). The other types of scale listed above require a lot of technical and professional input before they are used on the general public and in research.

### Advantages and disadvantages of using psychological tests and scales

**Advantages:** Tests give the researcher a standard procedure so that all participants can be treated in almost exactly the same way. Some psychologists would argue that this leads to greater reliability in results. Tests can be administered quickly and efficiently to many participants at once. Participants need not feel intimidated by the presence of a live interviewer and data collection cannot be distorted by the personal variables present when two people interact in an interview. However, where a questionnaire is administered in an interview type situation some influence from interpersonal variables is still possible.

**Disadvantages:** Tests do not gather the kind of deep and personally meaningful data produced by the semi-structured interview method described in Chapter 1. Being more similar to an examination than an interview, they can also be more intimidating if respondents feel they are being *evaluated* (see above). Technically, only information predetermined by the questionnaire or scale items, can be gathered. Participants may misinterpret items but this may not be apparent in the data analysis.

## Conclusions

There are a multitude of ways in which research studies, trying to measure variables, differences and effects, might be biased and give misleading results. We have highlighted only a few major sources and possible solutions for the problems raised.

Researchers will never get perfect measures or absolutely certain effects in a science which is inexact because there are a vast number of ever changing variables. Nevertheless, whenever we conduct a research project, no matter how small, we should always consider very carefully all the possible snags and biases, *before starting to collect our data*. Recognising problems at a later stage is simply too late.

# Summary

- We have looked at possible biases from **samples** of people, in particular the need for a **representative sample** and the meaning of a **random sample**, where all have an equal chance of being included.
- We also examined **stratified samples** (which take population proportions into account), **systematic sampling** (taking every nth person), **self-selecting samples** (e.g. volunteers), **opportunity samples** (by far the most common – who we can get) and **snowball samples** (use of key contacts).
- We then saw that the **expectations** that experimenters have about their research can influence the outcome of their studies. Such expectations may be controlled to some extent by using **blind procedures** and **reliability** checks.
- Participants too might influence results by having expectations about outcomes. They are influenced, no matter what the researcher says, by **demand characteristics** which give them cues to the true research hypothesis.
- Participants are **reactive** when they know they are being studied and may try to please the experimenter, be a good participant and/or try to look good in general (**social desirability**).
- Many of these effects can be minimised by the use of **standardised procedures**, use of a lie scale in questionnaires or simply by using a research design where participants do not

know that they are the object of study, though this carries ethical implications.

- **Questionnaires** are seen by many psychologists as 'instruments' which measure characteristics, skills, attitudes, aptitudes and abilities. These must be **standardised** (to make fair comparison between individuals and groups), **reliable** (consistent) and **valid** (measure what they say they do).

- Tests and scales are good for statistical comparison and hypothesis testing but can be criticised for giving rather narrow assessments of people and missing rich and unique aspects of people's experience.

# STATISTICS FOR DESCRIBING DATA

## 4

## Introduction

Statistical methods are used for two common purposes: first, *summarising* data (descriptive statistics) because there are usually far too many raw data to present to a reader of our report; second, statistics are used for deciding when two samples or scores are different enough to support the view that they come from different underlying populations. This is the sort of assessment we make when we argue that our study performance must have risen significantly, since our essay marks are *much* higher (not just a little) than they were last year. This second purpose is known as *significance testing* (inferential statistics) and we shall tackle this type in Chapter 5.

In this chapter, we look at the several ways in which data can be summarised for a reader to be able to grasp quickly what it is we wish to tell them about our research results. There are accepted ways and there are very poor ways to display such data. Poor ways are often used by the media, politicians and charlatans to try to convince us that an effect is real (for instance, that crime rates have risen dramatically or that a mystical healing process really works). Psychologists should present data only in terms of what gives the clearest, least ambiguous picture of what was found in a research study. Furthermore *raw data* (the scores gained by participants for instance) should be kept available for other researchers to investigate should they wish to challenge the research findings.

## What are descriptive statistics?

Quantitative data are some form of numerical description of events in the world. If you count sheep or measure your waistline you have reduced the fullness of an event to just the feature you wish to record. You extract just this information for a purpose

– you need to know if they will all fit into your sheep transporter or you wonder if you will get into a dress that is on sale. You have ignored the woolliness, cute eyes and noise of the sheep; you have ignored the roundness and colour of your waist. These features are irrelevant to your purpose.

In psychological research the same process occurs. In a memory recall test, we count words recalled and we might ignore the order of recall, the clustering of items (for instance, 'drink' was recalled together with 'ice' and 'glass') and the humour expressed by our participant in telling you the associations that helped them recall some of the words. What is important in this discussion is to note that measured data are an abstraction from events and that you, the measurer, have a choice as to how much information to extract and in what detail to record. Once you have made your decision and taken your measures you are stuck with that information and no more. One cannot usually go back and take further measurements.

# Types of data

## Categorical variables: nominal level data

Take a look at the items in Table 4.1 taken from a fictitious questionnaire. For the first two we can only choose one answer from a set of separate categories. There are no values in between and there is no particular order to the categories. The data we would obtain from 100 people would come as frequencies, for instance, 5 vegans, 35 vegetarians and 60 meat eaters (ignoring those who sometimes change their habits). We cannot separate the 35 vegetarians from one another; this is all we know because this is all we asked. Such variables are said to be *categorical*. If we give a code to each category, as we need to if we are to enter them into a spreadsheet, then the codes are said to be *nominal* data, that is, the number '1' given to the vegans does not measure anything which is three times less than the '3' given to meat eaters. The numbers are just *names* for categories, hence the term nominal.

Many independent variables are categorical in nature, e.g. with and without an audience, anagrams of concrete and abstract words, and so on.

## Measured variables: ordinal level data

Where we *can* separate people from one another by their positions on a variable we say that the variable is *measured* in some way. For instance, the numbers that people provide in answer to Items 3 and 4 of Table 4.1 separate them from each other along a single dimension. So do the numbers given as answers to Items 5 and 6. However, the numbers for Items 3 and 4 have a particular weakness as measures. For Item 3 we cannot sensibly say

**Table 4.1** *Items from a fictitious questionnaire*

**Item 1**

**Do you have many sleepless nights?**
 yes/no

**Item 2**

**How would you classify yourself as an eater:**
 vegan          vegetarian          meat eater

**Item 3**

**Cats can sometimes understand exactly what you are saying.**

| 1 | 2 | 3 | 4 | 5 | 6 | 7 |
|---|---|---|---|---|---|---|
| very strongly agree | strongly agree | agree | undecided | disagree | strongly disagree | very strongly disagree |

**Item 4**

**Please mark on the scale below the extent to which you experience pressure at work:**

No real pressure                                Highly pressured

0 ▬▬▬▬▬▬▬▬▬▬▬▬▬▬▬▬▬▬▬▬▬▬▬▬▬▬▬▬ 100

**Item 5**

**What is your height in centimetres?** ................ cms.

**Item 6**

**Name as many animals with tails as you can in the next 60 seconds.**

that, if I score 6, I am twice as disbelieving as someone who scores 3. What we can do is to put the responses *in order*. I am certainly further to the right-hand side of the scale than someone who scores 3. Similarly, looking at responses to Item 4, since the assessment is a quite subjective human judgement, we cannot say that someone choosing 80 is twice as pressured as someone choosing 40. What we can do is to rank people's scores as has been done in Table 4.2. The rank values in the second column are known as a set of *ordinal data* – these are always a set of ranks obtained by ordering a set of values. Note that the lowest rank is always given to the lowest value. Tied scores 'share' the ranks so that the two scores of 65 'share' the ranks 4 and 5 and so each receives the average of these two ranks (4.5).

**Table 4.2**    *Rank ordering of scores on item 4 in Table 1*

| Rating of pressure at work: | Rank: |
| --- | --- |
| 40 | 1 |
| 45 | 2 |
| 56 | 3 |
| 65 | 4.5 |
| 65 | 4.5 |
| 73 | 6 |
| 80 | 7 |

## Measured variables: interval level data

Values like those given as answers to Items 5 and 6 in Table 4.1 are said to be on an *interval scale of measurement*. There should be equal intervals between each position on such a scale. Standard measures of physical quantities, such as height, weight and time, are made on an interval scale. Scores on *standardised* psychological tests are also usually treated as being interval level data although the idea of equal intervals on an IQ scale, for instance, is dubious. Interval scales with a real zero starting point, such as height in cms or seconds taken to read a piece of text, are also often known as *ratio scales*. However, psychologists rarely if ever need to make this distinction when analysing their data and so we need only distinguish here between interval and ordinal level data.

These various levels of measurement are important when deciding which test of significance is appropriate for your data (see page 141). In the descriptive statistics section which follows, the methods introduced are related to each of the data levels just described.

## Descriptive statistics – the techniques used

Descriptive statistics are simply *measures used to describe a data set by summarising it in some general way*. Throughout this section it is worth remembering that the summary of data you provide is usually intended for a distant reader. They should be able to understand, *with no further questions necessary*, what it is you are trying to tell them about your gathered data set. In some ways this is an activity you are already used to performing, at least informally, because we all do this very frequently in everyday life. How would you describe your sleep pattern to your doctor? You might say something like 'Well, I tend to get around seven hours' sleep a night but near exams and assignment deadlines I drop to six-ish and on weekends I really lie-in and get about ten hours, I suppose'.

You have just provided a *summary* of many items of data. The two things we usually want to know about a set of data are their:

*central tendency* – the typical or fairly central value;
*dispersion* – to what extent the data are spread out around this central point.

In the example above you gave seven hours as your 'average', roughly central or typical value. You also gave some idea of the extent to which your nightly hours of sleep might vary, or be *dispersed* around this central value.

## Central tendencies

### Mode

The *mode* is simply the most frequent value in a set. The modal value in Table 4.3 is 3. The modal value you might obtain if you asked many UK families how many children they had, would probably be two. When we earlier talked of five vegans, 35 vegetarians and 60 meat eaters, the modal value, or rather *modal category*, is 'meat-eater'. Note the value is *not* 60 – this is the *frequency* obtained *in* the modal category.

**Table 4.3** *Number of errors made by 13 participants*

| 2 | 3 | 3 | 3 | 3 | 5 | 6 | 7 | 8 | 8 | 8 | 9 | 9 |
|---|---|---|---|---|---|---|---|---|---|---|---|---|

**Strengths and weaknesses:** the mode is very unreliable as a measure in a small data set. For instance, we only need two more 8s, above, for the modal value to change to 8 and only one more 8 for the set to have two modal values (the set becomes *bi-modal*). The mode is most useful when dealing with large data sets, as in a survey, especially where data are gathered in *categories*.

### Median

The *median* is the *central value* in a data set and is an *ordinal* measure. We find the median's *position* in a set by calculating $(n + 1)/2$. $n$ is the number of values in the set; in the set given in Table 4.3 there are 13 values, so $(13 + 1)/2 = 7$ and our median is in the seventh position, so its value is 6. If there is an even number of values our median is the average of the two central values, thus if $n = 10$ we get $(10 + 1)/2 = 5.5$, and this tells us that our median is the average of the fifth and sixth values. It is important to note that the median is the middle score of the set once the set has been ordered. The set above are already in order. In the set:

| 2 | 1 | 6 | 9 | 7 | 3 |
|---|---|---|---|---|---|

the median is the average of 3 and 6 (4.5). This is the average of the two middle scores, once the set has been put in numerical order.

**Strengths and weaknesses:** the median is a lot more representative of central values than the mode can be when we are dealing with small data sets. It is not distorted by extreme values in one direction, as is the *mean* (see below). However, it can be affected by skewed data (also see below) and where scores are rather *polarised*. For instance the median of:

| 1 | 3 | 5 | 7 | 23 | 35 | 46 |

is seven and this is obviously rather misleading.

## Mean

The *mean* as a measure of central tendency is what most people understand by the term 'average', even though there are various kinds of 'average' which is not a technically precise term. However, the mean *does* have a precise calculation. It can be found using the following formula:

$$\bar{x} = \frac{\Sigma x}{N}$$

The symbol for the mean is $\bar{x}$ and it is found by adding up all the scores (each one a value of 'x'; $\Sigma$ means add up each of what follows) and dividing by the number of scores there are. This is what you do to calculate how much each person should pay when you have all decided to share the costs of a meal or holiday. Here you are using a measure at *interval* level.

For the data in Table 4.3 we calculate:

$$2 + 3 + 3 + 3 + 3 + 5 + 6 + 7 + 8 + 8 + 8 + 9 + 9 = 74$$

$$\frac{74}{13} = \mathbf{5.69}$$

**Strengths and weaknesses:** the mean is the most *sensitive* measure, which is good in that it represents the exact centre point of all data points. However, it is easily distorted by a few 'rogue' scores in one direction. For example, the mean of 1, 3, 4, 5, 7 and 64 is 14, which is higher than five out of the six values in the set. The median here would be a more representative 4.5. The mean can also be a peculiar measure where original scores can only be whole numbers. We get, for instance, the famous average of 2.4 children per family!

## Measures of dispersion

We have so far looked just at the average, the typicality or the central point of a set of scores. This information is often not sufficient. We very often also need to know how far scores are *spread out* around the central point. For instance, if you were told that the average journey time from one part of the country to another is three hours, and yet your train took nearly four hours, you would not be too pleased to be told that this is quite within the 'normal range' – some journeys taking up to four hours and others only two! You would want to know that besides taking an average of three hours the dispersion of times was narrowly spread around that time.

So we need dispersion as well as central tendency, because we need to know how two sets of values differ even when they have much the same mean (see Figure 4.1). A memory experiment might produce roughly the same mean number of words correctly recalled from a list of 30, in two different conditions. However, it would be important to know that memory technique A produces a far narrower variation in scores than does memory technique B. This might indicate that the first method is a far more reliable and consistent approach for most people.

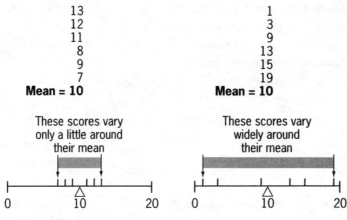

**Figure 4.1**  *Variation of two sets of scores around a mean of 10*

## The range

This measure is simply the distance between the top and bottom scores in a set, and can be used at ordinal or interval level. In Table 4.3 it is therefore the distance between 2 and 9. Now what is that distance? You might be tempted to say seven, and in everyday measurement this would be an adequate response. However, if we are talking of ordinal data, the ranks 2 to 9 include eight positions, not seven (think of the length of a set of bricks numbered 2 to 9; the range is 8 bricks). On an interval scale, measuring to the nearest centimetre, '2 cm' means anything between 1.5 cm and 2.5 cm. The range 2 cm to 9 cm then *could* be, at the extreme, 1.5 cm to 9.5 cm = 8 cm.

Hence the simple formula for the range is:

$$\text{range} = \text{top value} - \text{bottom value} + 1$$

**Strengths and weaknesses:** the range tells us the entire spread of scores in a set, but it tells us nothing about the way in which scores are spread out *within* that range.

## The variation ratio

This measure is used with data which have been treated as *frequencies* (i.e. nominal level), where the *mode* was used for the central tendency. It is the number of items not in the modal category compared with the total number of items. In other words it is the answer to the question 'What proportion were not in the most populated category?'

In Table 4.3 there are 13 values and four of these are in the modal group. Hence:

$$\text{Variation ratio} = \frac{\text{number of non-modal values}}{\text{total number of values}}$$

$$= \frac{9}{13} = \textbf{0.69} \text{ (or 0.7)}$$

**Strengths and weaknesses:** the variation ratio is useful for telling us how representative the mode is of all values. It is unaffected by extreme variations in scores. However, like the range, it tells us nothing about how spread out or condensed our set of scores is. It also tells us nothing about the overall range.

### The standard deviation

This statistic can cause some pain and a lot of confusion so we shall take it slowly, one step at a time.

Suppose your class had just been given a revision test and that the mean score in the group, was 55 out of 100. Suppose you proudly announce to parent (or boy/girl friend) 'The mean was 55 and I got 65'. This might be very good indeed from your point of view. On the other hand it could be that yours is the next score above the mean and that many people in the class were higher than 65. We cannot tell how good your performance was because we know nothing about how the scores are spread around the mean. Note that the range tells us nothing helpful here and the variation ratio would tell us nothing at all about your particular score. We need something that tells us whether you are close to or far from the mean relative to other people.

**Deviation:** is the distance of your score from the mean. This should be fairly easy to calculate. We simply take the mean score from your score ($x - \bar{x}$, where $x$ is your score). This gives us a value $d$, called a **deviation score**. Now, if we calculate $d$ for every value in the set what we then need is some kind of **average** of these deviations in order to know how everybody else is placed around the mean and to know whether a deviation of ten is a very good result or close to an average result (see Figure 4.2).

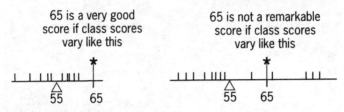

65 is a very good score if class scores vary like this

65 is not a remarkable score if class scores vary like this

55   65

55   65

**Figure 4.2** *Variation among scores tells us how good a particular score is*

So we need some measure of the **typical** deviation. We could take the mean of all deviations, but the result would be zero because half the deviations are negative (because they are below the mean) and half positive. A statistic known as the **mean deviation** is the mean of all deviations **ignoring their sign** (so negative deviations are treated as if they are positive).

However, in statistical work an extremely common, useful and powerful measure of dispersion is the **standard deviation**. The formula for this is:

$$s = \sqrt{\left[\frac{\Sigma d^2}{N-1}\right]}$$

Since $d$ is $x - \bar{x}$, the full version of this formula is:

$$s = \sqrt{\left[\frac{\Sigma(x - \bar{x})^2}{N-1}\right]}$$

Although this may look forbidding, all we actually have to do here is square each deviation, add up all the results, divide by $N - 1$ and find the square root of this result. The result at the stage before this (i.e. before taking the final square root) is known as the **variance** ($s^2$) and you will often find this referred to in more advanced discussions of statistics. The calculation steps for standard deviation are shown in Box 4.1.

**Box 4.1** *Calculating the standard deviation*

Let's suppose we want to find the standard deviation of the class scores in the left-hand column below:

**Steps in calculation**

1 Find the mean; = 14
2 take the mean from each score in order to obtain each person's *deviation* score; see column 2
3 square results of step 2 see column 3;
4 add all results of step 3;

| Score (x) | x − x̄ (= x − 14) | (x − x̄)² |
|-----------|------------------|-----------|
| 16 | 2 | 4 |
| 19 | 5 | 25 |
| 12 | −2 | 4 |
| 10 | −4 | 16 |
| 14 | 0 | 0 |
| 13 | −1 | 1 |
| 17 | 3 | 9 |
| 18 | 4 | 16 |
| 10 | −4 | 16 |
| 11 | −3 | 9 |
| **140** | | **100** |

4 add all results of step 3;
$$= \Sigma(x - \bar{x})^2$$
$$= 100$$
5 divide result of step 4 by $N - 1$; $= \Sigma(x - \bar{x})^2/N-1$
$$= 11.11*$$
6 find square root of step 5

$$= \sqrt{\left( \frac{\Sigma(x - \bar{x})^2}{N - 1} \right)}$$
$$= 3.33$$

Sum $= 140$
$\bar{x} = 140/10$
$\bar{x} = 14$

$$S = \sqrt{\left( \frac{\Sigma(x - \bar{x})^2}{N-1} \right)} = \sqrt{\left( \frac{100}{9} \right)} = \sqrt{11.11} = 3.33$$

* Note that at this point we have the variance

The standard deviation is an interval level statistic used throughout the practice of significance testing, which we will encounter in Chapter 5. We can use the standard deviation of a *sample* to estimate the standard deviation of the *population* it came from, so long as it was drawn *at random* from that population. For instance, we can use a *sample* standard deviation to estimate the dispersion of reading scores for *all* eight-year-olds, so long as we take a good, representative sample (see page 52) from that population. This is why issues of sampling are so important. Also, because the standard deviation is used to estimate statistical features of populations, $N - 1$ is used in the formula above, rather than $N$ which would give the exact mean of squared deviations. The $N - 1$ makes the standard deviation a little bit larger in order to allow for error in making estimations from smaller samples.

**Standard scores (or z score): z** is *the number of standard deviations any particular score is from the mean.* In other words, to find someone's z score we simply divide their deviation score by the standard deviation. The person with a score of 19 in Box 4.1 has a deviation score of 5. How many standard deviations is this from the mean? To find out we have to divide the individual deviation by the standard deviation, (i.e. 5/3.3 = 1.52). This person's z score is 1.52. They are 1.52 **z**s from the mean.

**Strengths and weaknesses:** the standard deviation, unlike the other measures of dispersion covered here, *does* give an indication of how condensed or spread out all the values are around the mean of a set. However, like the mean it is also distorted by extreme values in one direction. Its main strength is in the power it gives, in more advanced statistics, to make statistical estimates of populations from which samples have been drawn.

## Frequencies

Suppose we ask a sample of 48 students to state their religion (if any) and we get the set of data shown below where C = Christian, Ca = Catholic, H = Hindu, M = Muslim, J = Jew, S = Sikh, O = other, U = unsure about this and D = don't believe in any religion:

CCCCaCaHHHMMMCCMJJJSSOOOOUUMUUDDDD
MMMJJJHHCaCaCaCCDDO        (N = 48)

As we have seen earlier in the chapter, the only descriptive statistics we can use on these (that we have covered so far) are the mode and variation ratio. These would tell us that Muslim is the modal category and that 40/48, or 0.83, is the variation ratio. This does not really tell us a lot about the data set. If we wish to give our reader some idea of the *distribution* of responses we can draw up a *frequency table* as shown in Table 4.4.

**Table 4.4** *Frequencies of religions for a sample of students*

| Christian | Catholic | Hindu | Muslim | Jew | Sikh | Other | Unsure | Don't believe | Total |
|-----------|----------|-------|--------|-----|------|-------|--------|---------------|-------|
| 7 | 5 | 5 | 8 | 6 | 2 | 5 | 4 | 6 | 48 |

If we ask people to respond on *two* variables we can draw up the sort of '2 × 2' table shown in the next chapter as Table 5.6, where people have been asked whether they are for or against animal testing for cosmetic products *and* whether or not they are a student. If we had asked *three* groups (students, lecturers and administration staff) we would have ended up with a '2 × 3' table, and so on.

## Graphical display

Another way to summarise data for the reader is to make a graphical display or chart. Note that these are always known as 'figures' in a research report and should be numbered consecutively, as in this book.

Here are some dos and don'ts about charts:

- **Do** provide a title and labels for each axis of your chart so that a naive reader can understand it without referring to your text.
- **Do** make sure your Y axis starts from zero or is 'cut' (as in Figure 4.4) to show that it doesn't, otherwise your chart can be very misleading.
- **Don't** make a chart showing each participant's score or value – this is not a *summary* of the data set and it produces unruly bars in an arbitrary order.
- **Don't** rely on computer drawn charts unless you fully understand what they are saying. They will only pick up the labels you have used in the spreadsheet and some packages 'cheat' by not starting the Y axis from zero, for instance.
- **Don't** go mad with pretty colours. These can be distracting and they will not gain you any extra marks in assignment work! Use black, and a minimum of shading only as necessary for communication.

## *The bar chart*

We can plot the frequencies shown in Table 4.4 as the bar chart shown in Figure 4.3.

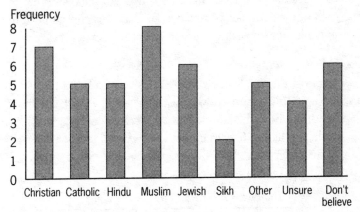

Category of religion stated by participants

**Figure 4.3** *Frequencies of religions for a sample of 48 students*

You should note especially the following points:

- The bars are separated here because the variable on the x-axis (types of religion) is a *categorical variable*. There is no logical *ordering* of these categories.

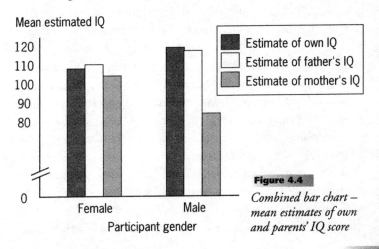

**Figure 4.4**

*Combined bar chart – mean estimates of own and parents' IQ score*

- The bars *could* represent proportions (such as percentages) or other similar statistical properties such as the mean scores in conditions or groups. Figure 4.4 shows the means produced by participants asked to estimate their own IQ score and that of each of their parents. In this type of chart it is conventional to put columns for each sub-group adjacent to each other.

## The histogram

In a histogram we plot *only* frequencies of scores of a measured variable. A histogram shows the shape of the *distribution* of scores throughout the sample taken. On rare occasions this is for a whole population (e.g. exam marks of *all* students in a college).

If we collect the data shown in Table 4.3 into a frequency table we get Table 4.5.

**Table 4.5**  *Data from Table 4.3 in frequencies*

| Number of errors: | 2 | 3 | 4 | 5 | 6 | 7 | 8 | 9 |
|---|---|---|---|---|---|---|---|---|
| Frequency: | 1 | 4 | 0 | 1 | 1 | 1 | 3 | 2 |

A histogram for these frequencies is shown in Figure 4.5. You should note the following points in particular:

- Frequencies for the whole of the data set are shown.
- Empty values within the overall range must be shown, hence a gap appears for the value '4', indicating that no one correctly recalled just four words. The frequency for '4' is zero.
- The columns must be the same width for the same size interval.
- If columns are all the same width then the area of each one represents the proportion of the whole who are represented by that column. Hence, four people made three errors and these are represented by a column which is 4/13 of the total area 'under the curve'. (Statisticians talk of the area 'under the curve', although the shape enclosed by the columns in Figure 4.5 is not exactly a curve. You will see shortly that large distributions of frequencies do usually form a curve.)
- Other than empty values, the overall shape of the curve is continuous; columns are not separated as in a bar chart.

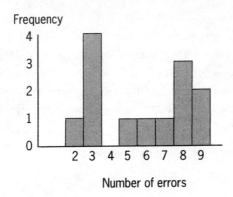

**Figure 4.5** *Histogram – frequency of errors made by 13 participants*

## The frequency polygon

There is another popular way to draw a frequency histogram like that in Figure 4.5; this is to plot the same data as a frequency polygon, shown in Figure 4.6. You should note here that:

- The points of the frequency polygon are the mid-points of the top of each column on the regular histogram (see Figure 4.5).
- Where possible the polygon is completed at each end by drawing a line down to touch the x-axis at the mid-point of the next (empty) column.

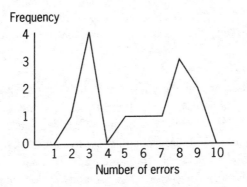

**Figure 4.6** *Frequency polygon – frequency of errors made by 13 participants*

## Line chart

In *time-series studies,* where groups of people or animals are measured at regular intervals, it is common to draw a line chart of the resulting set of scores over time. Such a chart could be drawn for the (fictitious) growth in vocabulary over the first two years at school, of children who have and have not attended a pre-school nursery – see Figure 4.7.

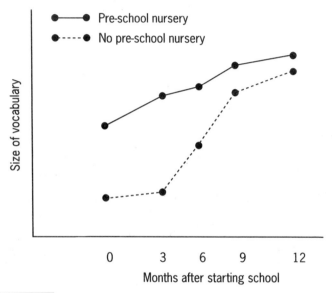

**Figure 4.7** *Line chart – development of vocabulary over first year of schooling by children with and without pre-school nursery experience*

## Stem and leaf chart

Despite the warning above about not drawing a chart with a bar for every individual's score, there is one special kind of histogram-like figure which *will* both summarise a data set of scores in an organised manner, yet still show us every individual score value. This is one of a set of methods introduced by Tukey (1977) and generally known as methods of 'exploratory data analysis'. The data on the left of Figure 4.8 produce the *stem and leaf chart* shown to the right of the figure. The 'stem' in this case shows intervals of ten. The 'leaves' are the unit digits of each score. Hence, '4' under the stem heading represents 40 and the scores of 41, 41 and 45 are shown by simply entering 1, 1 and 5 as 'leaves'. The usefulness of this type of chart is that one can see at a glance, as in a histogram, what *shape* the scores take and whether there are any obvious skews (see below) while at the same time being able to see just how many of each type of score there are in each interval (column).

**Score**
3
5
11
14
16
16
19
21
23
23
25
27
33
35
36
37
41
41
45

The scores to the left form the stem and the leaf chart shown below. See text for explanation.

| Stem | Leaf |
|------|------|
| 0 | 35 |
| 1 | 14669 |
| 2 | 13357 |
| 3 | 3567 |
| 4 | 115 |

**Figure 4.8**  *Stem and leaf chart*

## The normal distribution – a special type of histogram

Suppose we had developed a test for anxiety with 20 items, to each of which respondents could respond with 'always', 'often', 'sometimes' or 'never', for which they score 1, 2, 3 or 4. This is true of Spielberger's trait anxiety test (Spielberger *et al.*, 1983). Therefore total scores on this test can range from 20 to 80. We might draw up a frequency distribution histogram for these scores looking something like Figure 4.9. We would find that very few people score extremely high and very few get an extremely low score. Most people would be somewhere in the middle. The mean value might be 45 as indicated on the figure.

A figure such as Figure 4.9 can be said to approximate to a curve very familiar to statisticians, known as the *normal distribution*. One of these is shown in Figure 4.10. The curve is called 'normal' for purely *mathematical* reasons (you may remember the use of the term 'normal' as meaning 'perpendicular' in geometry). Do note that the *actual* distribution curves that occur for psychological data, and most other physical measurements, only ever *approximate* to a normal curve. However, they are often so close to the pure normal distribution curve that on most occasions the difference between actual curve and theoretical curve is insignificant and we may treat data as though they form a perfect, normal distribution.

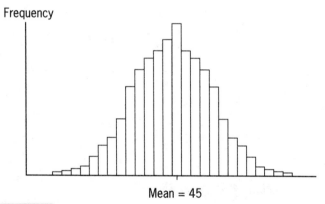

Mean = 45

**Figure 4.9** *Likely distribution of scores, for a large sample, on a test of anxiety*

### Characteristics of a normal distribution curve:

1 It is symmetrical about the mid-point of the horizontal axis;
2 The point about which it is symmetrical (the line marked 'M' in Figure 4.10) is the point at which the mean, median and mode all fall;
3 We know what percentage of the area under the curve is contained between the mean and the point where one standard deviation falls (or indeed two or three standard deviations – see Figure 4.12).

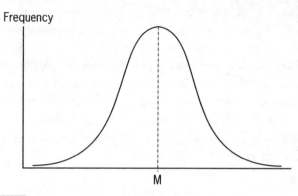

**Figure 4.10** *A normal distribution*

In fact, if we know how many standard deviations a score is from the mean (that is its *z* score – see page 83), we can work out the area between that score and the mean. We can also therefore work out the percentage of people who would fall above and below that score. In Figure 4.11 we have a distribution of scores on a reading test where the mean of a large sample of scores is 40 and the standard deviation is 10. Obviously, 50 per cent of people fall below 40 and 50 per cent are above 40. The top 50 per cent of scores is shaded in the figure. It is known that, *on any*

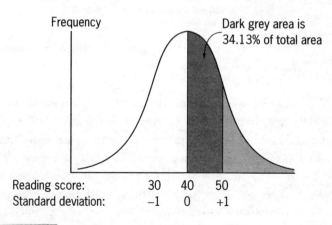

**Figure 4.11** *Proportions above and below a score*

*normal distribution,* one standard deviation ($z$ = +1) cuts off roughly the top 16 per cent of values and it occurs at the position shown by the line above 50 in Figure 4.11. This is the point where the downward curve inflects from an inward to an outward direction. The area between the mean and this line is therefore around 34 per cent of the whole (50–16 per cent), and is shown in darker grey. From this we know that 34 per cent of children score between 40 and 50 points on this test, since the standard deviation is 10 points.

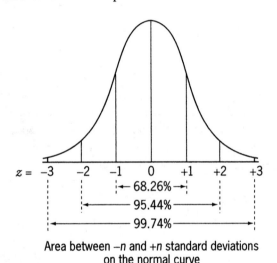

Area between –*n* and +*n* standard deviations
on the normal curve

**Figure 4.12** *Proportions of a normal distribution between* n *standard deviations*

This kind of knowledge about data which form a normal distribution is very important in the area of significance testing (see Chapter 5) and in the construction of psychological tests. Note that the proportions given in Figure 4.12 apply *no matter what are the actual mean and standard deviation for a population of scores.* Because of the properties of the normal distribution and its value in statistical estimations, constructors of psychological tests try to create tests that produce a normal distribution of scores when they are tested on large, representative samples of people. Such tests are said to be *standardised to a normal distribution*. Note this means that, unlike physical properties of people (such as height and heart rate), measured psychological qualities such as self-esteem and extroversion and even IQ come out normally distributed *because the tests were so constructed*. The psychological variables are assumed on theoretical grounds to be normally distributed but there is no independent way of asserting this as fact. In the case of arm length or lung capacity, the measures used (cm, cc.) exist independently of the need to measure arm length or lung capacity. These characteristics are normally distributed as a matter of established *fact*.

### Skewed distributions

Some distributions have an overall 'one hump' shape like the normal distribution but are *skewed* to one side because of the nature of the variable measure or test in use (see Figure 4.13). Reaction times are *positively skewed* because it is hard to go much faster than the mean value but it is much easier to be a lot slower on any one particular occasion – there is much more room to be slower. Hence a large sample of reaction times will include a 'tail' of slower times, as shown in Figure 4.13b.

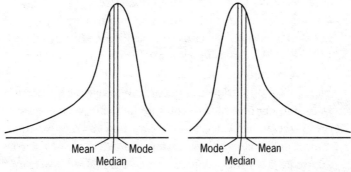

a) Negatively skewed distribution     b) Positively skewed distribution

**Figure 4.13**   *Skewed distributions – positive and negative*

# Conclusions

There are many ways in which we can summarise data but there are also several limitations. First, the *level of measurement* used may be restrictive. If the data gathering instrument was relatively crude (e.g. a 'yes/no' answer) then we cannot extract more subtle data – we can simply count frequencies. So, long before reaching the stage of statistical analysis, at the point where we *construct* measures, we should pay careful attention to what we eventually want our data to show. Second, there are limitations in terms of what is useful and clear to our readers. Finally, there are limitations concerning what is *legitimate* or *fair* in our presentation of data.

# Summary

- We looked first at the **level of measurement** of data, dividing measures initially into those that are **categorical** and those that are on a **measured scale**.

- Measured scales were divided into **ordinal scales** (where values are only in rank order) and **interval scales** (where values are placed on a scale with equal intervals).

- We then examined how data can be summarised in terms of their typical or middle value – their **central tendency** – and in terms of the spread of scores – **dispersion**.

- Measures of central tendency are: **mode** (most frequent value); **median** (central ranked value); **mean** (arithmetic average), with the latter being most subtle but also the most sensitive to extreme values.

- Measures of dispersion are: **range** (top to bottom); **variation ratio** (ratio of non-modal scores to the total); **variance** (average of the squared deviations); **standard deviation** (square root of the variance). A **deviation** is the distance of a particular score from the group mean and a **standard score**, or *z* **score**, is the number of standard deviations a particular score is from the mean.

- **Frequencies** are what we obtain if we count the number of occurrences in any category we use to record observations.
- A graphical display of all frequencies is a **histogram**, a special kind of **bar chart**.
- Bar charts consist of bars representing selected means, proportions, frequencies etc., but histograms show only frequencies, and **all** the frequencies in a data set.
- The **frequency polygon** is another form of histogram, made by joining the mid-points of the frequency columns in the corresponding histogram.
- A **line chart** displays a series of measures from the same individual or group, often comparing two or more sets of measures as two or more lines.
- A **stem and leaf** chart is a form of **exploratory data analysis** which combines features of a histogram with a depiction of all the raw data in a set.
- A **normal distribution** possesses well-understood and useful mathematical features; it is the shape taken up by measures of many natural human characteristics. Constructors of psychological tests attempt to make their psychological measures produce a normal distribution, so that statistical values for the relevant whole population are relatively easy to estimate.
- A **skewed distribution** has more scores to one side of the mode than the other.

# STATISTICS FOR TESTING HYPOTHESES

**5**

## Introduction

Significance testing is the process of deciding whether to accept a result (a difference) as a large enough one to take seriously or whether to dismiss the result, as probably the result *only* of random variables or *sampling error*. In everyday language we might say that it only 'occurred by chance'. The same issue arises for correlations; is the extent to which two variables change together just coincidental or shall we assume that there is something behind the relationship? In testing hypotheses (for example whether music improves language learning) we have to decide between two possibilities. Either the difference between two sets of language test scores (with and without music) is the size we would expect quite often between any two sets of test scores (therefore 'not significant'), or the difference is unlikely to have occurred on such a 'chance' basis – in which case we accept it as a *significant difference*. This is known as a *significance decision*.

## Significance decisions

Let's demonstrate the making of a significance decision with an everyday example and then look at an example in psychological research.

**At the greengrocer's:** suppose you ask the greengrocer for an avocado pear. You have had an argument with him in previous weeks about his short measures, but when you take all your shopping home you are dismayed to find that the avocado is very much on the small side. 'You'd get a load of those in a pound' you remark to yourself before remembering that the shopkeeper had a new box on display labelled 'baby avocados'. Back at the shop you argue that you must have been given one of those baby fruits by mistake. The shopkeeper is a rather mean character, clearly not perturbed by the threat of losing your trade, and maintains that the pear is just a rather small one, selected at random from the 'normal' box. You argue that, given the range of sizes in the normal box, the likelihood of picking one this small is so low that you are inclined to believe it was a random selection from the 'baby' box, (and probably done because of your previous arguments). So, the greengrocer is saying that your avocado varies at a chance level from the mean 'normal' size, whereas you're saying that it varies too far from the 'normal' mean to be just 'chance' variation. Which possibility shall we choose as true? This is the fundamental decision to be made when conducting a statistical significance test.

**How much blame?** Now let us suppose your psychology tutor asks you to carry out a research assignment in which you have to investigate the extent to which people are affected by the seriousness of a road accident when they attribute responsibility to the driver. In one condition people are told that the consequences of an accident were 'light' (a damaged bumper), while in the other condition they are told the consequences are 'serious' (one person taken to hospital with non-fatal injuries). Suppose the results gained in this experiment were as shown in Table 5.1. Here we have the same decision to make about whether the outcome (the difference in responsibility rating between the light and serious conditions) is one where we should say only random variation is at work or one where we say the difference is *significant*, that is, we would take the results as support for the theory that perceived responsibility varies with the seriousness of an accident. What we are asking, in effect, is 'can we dismiss this difference as what is to be expected just by chance variation between identical conditions' or 'shall we take this difference as reflecting a *real* difference between conditions?'

**Table 5.1** *Ratings of responsibility (1 = not responsible to 20 = completely responsible) for a driver in an accident with 'light' and 'serious' consequences*

One would not normally work with samples as small as this but the number is kept low here to make the demonstration easier with small size calculations.

| Consequences of accident | |
|---|---|
| a light | b serious |
| 1 | 8 |
| 7 | 12 |
| 5 | 12 |
| 11 | 13 |
| 9 | 18 |

This second situation is rather like, in the previous example, having not just one avocado but two *samples* of avocados and trying to decide whether they were *both* taken from the 'normal size' box or whether one came from one box and one from the other. This is how you should always think of any two sets of scores you obtain in a psychology investigation. They are *samples* drawn from *populations*. In the case of the accident responsibility ratings, the 'population' is not people or fruits but an infinite set of scores we could obtain by running this experiment over and over again.

## Null and alternative hypotheses

It is time to move towards a little more formality with our terms. In a significance test we have to decide between the truth of two possibilities. Either:

- the two samples of scores are drawn from the same population (or two identical populations);

or

- the two samples are drawn from two different populations.

The first of these is known as a *null hypothesis* and is written for short as $H_0$. There are several features of a null hypothesis:

- It is a hypothesis based on the concept of no difference – nothing is 'going on'.
- In tests of difference it is the assumption that the two populations that samples have been drawn from are identical, or that they have the same mean.
- It is statistical and abstract – we could never show this kind of null hypothesis to be exactly true. In a significance test we simply *assume* it to be true.
- The null hypothesis is the hypothesis we would like to be able to reject at the end of a research study; we would like to reject $H_0$ in favour of the alternative hypothesis $(H_1)$ – that the two populations are different or have different means.

An *alternative hypothesis* $(H_1)$ has the following properties:

- The *alternative hypothesis* is the one we usually want to emerge as the 'better bet'. We want to show that it is more reasonable to assume the alternative hypothesis is correct than to assume the null hypothesis is correct.
- The alternative and null hypotheses are complimentary. Each one covers every possibility that the other does not; either there is no difference between the two populations $(H_0)$ or there is $(H_1)$.

In the avocado example, the greengrocer was sticking with the null hypothesis whereas the customer was proposing the alternative hypothesis.

In the accident responsibility experiment, our null hypothesis is that the rating scores in column a and in column b of Table 5.1

come from identical populations. The assumption is that they are just two random selections from identical populations of scores or the same population. Let us see how we can move towards showing this is rather unlikely in this particular case.

# Significance testing and probability

In a significance test we:

- assume the *null hypothesis* is true;
- calculate the *probability* of getting our result *if the null hypothesis is true*;
- reject the null hypothesis if this probability is too small.

This is the equivalent of saying to the greengrocer that if the avocado was drawn from the 'normal size' box, the probability of doing so was very small and that therefore we are inclined towards the alternative hypothesis that it was drawn from the 'baby avocado' box.

In the accident responsibility experiment, how can we estimate the probability of our difference occurring if the null hypothesis is true?

Well, the first step is to treat our data as ordinal. We do this here partly for simplicity but also because we only asked participants to rate responsibility on a scale of one to 20 and we are certainly not using an equal interval scale in this case. We cannot claim that my 10 is twice your five. So we are safer treating the data as ordinal. The scores have therefore been ranked in columns c and d of Table 5.2. You can see that we rank all the scores as one set.

The reasoning now is that:

- if people give higher responsibility ratings in the 'serious' condition then ranks in this condition will be generally higher;
- if the 'serious' condition ranks are higher then the *rank total* for this condition will also be higher.

**Table 5.2**  *Ranks of the data in Table 1*

| Rating of responsibility in conditions: | | Rank of ratings in conditions: | | Minimum and maximum possible ranks | |
|---|---|---|---|---|---|
| a light | b serious | c light | d serious | e | f |
| 1 | 8 | 1 | 4 | 1 | 6 |
| 7 | 12 | 3 | 7.5 | 2 | 7 |
| 5 | 12 | 2 | 7.5 | 3 | 8 |
| 11 | 13 | 6 | 9 | 4 | 9 |
| 9 | 18 | 5 | 10 | 5 | 10 |
| Rank total $R_A = 17$ | | $R_B = 38$ | | 15 | 40 |

What we have found is that the rank total in the 'serious' condition is 38 whereas the 'light' condition rank total is only 17. What is the probability of this occurring if there really is no difference between conditions (that is, if $H_0$ is true)?

## Probability

Probability is measured on a scale of 0 to 1. Things that cannot possibly happen are given a probability of 0. However, there are very few occasions on which this can be said. Any event in the physical world has a finite probability of occurrence. Even the possibility that you will win the lottery has a value – although it is only 0.0000000714! Things that are very likely to happen have a probability value approaching one. At the start of the season, the probability that your favourite football team will score at least one goal during the season is very high indeed (but there is the very tiny probability that it might not!).

### Probability distributions

We can display probabilities as a distribution. Imagine we sat up all night taking two socks at a time from a drawer containing equal numbers of black and white socks. Figure 5.1 shows the likely frequency of drawing a matching pair or a mixed pair. In fact the

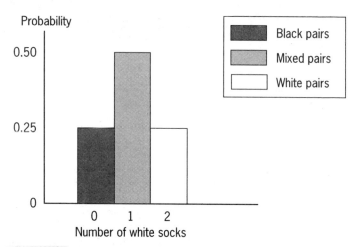

**Figure 5.1** *Probability of drawing matching or non-matching pairs from a drawer containing 50% black and 50% white socks*

chart is drawn as a *probability distribution* showing the theoretical probability associated with drawing each combination. Note that the four possible events that can occur here are: black + black, black + white, white + black and white + white. Hence, a mixed pair will occur *twice* as often as a matching *black* pair, but as often as a matching pair of *either colour*. We do not actually have to sit up all night to find out what would occur in practice. Over very many trials, the theoretical pattern in Figure 5.1 will emerge.

Now let's return to our accident responsibility results. In Table 5.2 what we are asking is: 'what is the probability that we would get a rank total as low as 17 in one condition, if the null hypothesis is true?'

The probability of an event occurring is calculated from:

$$\frac{\text{the number of ways the event can occur}}{\text{the total number of things that can happen altogether}}$$

From Figure 5.1, for example, we can see that the probability of drawing a pair of black socks at random is 0.25. This is because there are four possible outcomes, as we saw above, and we want just one of these. This gives ¼ or if you like, the 'odds' are 1 in 4. With the accident responsibility data, we want the probability of one group of five ranks being as low as 17. Imagine we drew five numbers at random from a hat containing the numbers 1 to 10, and repeated this selection many times. We add up the total of the five numbers each time and plot these as a frequency histogram. We would obtain the distribution shown in Figure 5.2. This shows us how often a rank total as low as 17 would occur 'by chance' in a random selection of five ranks from ten. The lowest total we *could* possibly get is 15, the highest is 40 (see columns **e** and **f** of Table 5.2). Hence, overall our frequency distribution would look something like Figure 5.2. Notice that a rank total of 15 occurs very rarely, as does a rank total of 40. The most frequent rank totals are the central ones on the chart (27 and 28). The totals fall in a distribution with a very similar shape to that of the *normal distribution* that we met in Chapter 4.

From this distribution, if we were mad enough to sit up all night producing it, we would be able to calculate the exact probability of obtaining a rank total of 17. Don't forget, this would be the probability of obtaining a rank total of 17 *if the null hypothesis is true*. If the null hypothesis is true then it is as if we are

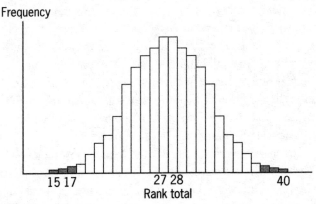

**Figure 5.2** *Distribution of rank totals obtained from repeated selection of five numbers from a hat containing 1 to 10*

selecting five ranks from 10 at random. We do not actually need to sit up all night however, since statisticians have invented formulae that give the probability distributions for obtaining particular results under the null hypothesis. Figure 5.2 shows that the sum of 5 ranks drawn randomly from 10 will very rarely be 17 or lower (or as high as 38).

Turning back to Figure 5.1 we see that the probability of drawing a black pair of socks is 0.25. Notice that this is the proportion of the whole area of this chart that the 'black pair' column takes up. Remember that the area of columns in a histogram represent the *proportion* that value takes of the whole (see page 86). Therefore, the probability of obtaining a rank total of 17 is the area that the column above 17 takes up of the whole area of Figure 5.2 (the third column from the left). We can see that this is a tiny area and therefore represents a very small probability.

## Statistical significance tests

To calculate the probability of obtaining a rank total as low as 17 for one group, when we have two groups of five, we can conduct a statistical significance test known as the Mann–Whitney test which we will calculate in detail a little later in this chapter.

There is a qualification to be added here, before proceeding. We do not actually want the probability of obtaining a rank total of *exactly* 17 for the lower total. We want the probability of obtaining a value of 17 *or lower*. This is because we want to know the probability, if the null hypothesis is true, of obtaining a rank total as low as ours. Obviously a rank total even lower than ours will also challenge the null hypothesis. We are interested in showing how unexpected are the events signified by the shaded area of the frequency distribution to the left in Figure 5.2.

If we were to perform the Mann–Whitney test on a computer program this would tell us that the probability of obtaining a result of 17 or lower is just 0.014. This means that there is only a 14/1000 chance of this happening *if the null hypothesis is true*. A result as extreme as this one (in our favour) would occur only 14 times in every 1000 times that a sample of five was randomly drawn from the numbers 1 to 10.

### One- and two-tailed tests

There is just one more qualification to be made now. We found above the probability of obtaining a result 'as extreme as ours' if the null hypothesis is true. The problem is that we only considered 'extreme' in one direction. It would be equally 'extreme' if the rank total for the 'light' group had been 38. However, it would be a big surprise since we thought that people would give a higher level of responsibility where more serious consequences have occurred. However, nothing can be ruled out in psychological research. Perhaps people feel very sympathetic for the driver under the cloud of having caused such injury and, because they think 'there but for the grace of God go I', might attribute a *reduced* level of responsibility. This seems very unlikely but statistically *anything* is possible. Hence, to be safe, many researchers conduct what are known as *two-tailed statistical tests*.

Two-tailed tests look at the probability of getting a result as extreme as the one found *in either direction*.

In this case we would look at the probability of getting a rank total of 17 or less, *or* a rank total of 38 or greater. Hence we need to add to our original result the probability of getting a rank total of 38, 39 or 40 (represented by the mirror-image shaded columns to the right of Figure 5.2). We just need to double the original probability of 0.014 and this gives us 0.028.

### Rejecting the null hypotheses

All right. So far we have found the probability of obtaining a difference as extreme as our one *if the null hypothesis is true*. This probability is very low. We have been saying that when the probability of getting results under $H_0$ is 'very low' we shall reject it, just as we rejected the greengrocer's claim that the avocado was selected from the 'normal size' box. But how low is 'very low'? We need to determine a cut-off point on Figure 5.2 where we would reject the null hypothesis if our result falls below that point.

Would we feel our case for the alternative hypothesis was strong if our difference fell in the most extreme 10% of random differences, the extreme 5% or perhaps only the extreme 1%? Let's find out what is the conventional practice among researchers.

---

**PAUSE FOR THOUGHT**

The most extreme 1%, 5% and 10% of a (normal) probability distribution are shown as shaded areas in Figure 5.3. When would you feel comfortable in saying that your result was so unlikely under the null hypothesis that the null hypothesis is probably wrong? If it fell in the most extreme 1%, 5% or 10%?

---

In social science a difference is said to be 'significant' when the probability of it occurring, if the null hypothesis is true, falls below 0.05.

This cut-off point is known as the '5% significance level'. Our responsibility experiment result certainly falls below this level. We had $p = 0.028$. Therefore we would be able to call our result a 'significant difference' and we would report this as being 'significant with $p < 0.05$'. [Note that 0.05 = 5%]

In a short while we shall see how we would come to this same conclusion working the Mann-Whitney test out by hand.

### The 5% significance level and one- and two-tailed tests

You may only conduct a one-tailed test where, *if* the result went in the *opposite direction* to that which you expected from your theory, you would not claim the result as 'significant'. In this case you consider the 5% of probabilities at the *predicted end of the distribution only*. If your result falls in the extreme 5% of values at the *opposite* end from where you expected, and you claim this as significant, then you are really saying that results are significant if they fall in the most extreme 10% of values. You will not be taken seriously by other researchers. In a one-tailed test even an extreme result in the wrong direction must be considered 'just chance'. Because this is so rarely likely to be the case in psychology studies, many researchers stick to the sole use of two-tailed tests no matter what the direction of the original hypothesis.

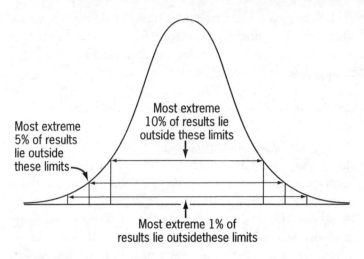

**Figure 5.3** *Most extreme areas of probability – 10%, 5% and 1% cut-off points*

## Type I and type II errors

Of course, even if we get a very extreme result under $H_0$, it could still be a fluke. If you were picking socks in the dark from the drawer described earlier and you happened to pick a black pair first time, you might conclude that the drawer is full of black socks. You would be rejecting the null hypothesis that there are, in fact, equal numbers of black and white socks. When this mistake occurs it is known as a type 1 error. A type II error is the mirror image – it occurs when we *retain* a null hypothesis (because we did not obtain a significant result) when, in fact, the alternative hypothesis is true. This would be like assuming that proportions

| | | Null hypothesis is: | |
|---|---|---|---|
| | | **Retained** | **Rejected** |
| **Null hypothesis** | **True** | ✓ | Type I error |
| **is actually:** | **False** | Type II error | ✓ |

**Table 5.3** *Type I and type II errors*

of black and white socks are equal because we drew a mixed pair, when, in fact, the drawer contains only a few white socks – but we were unlucky enough to have drawn one of these! The definitions of type I and type II errors are given in Table 5.3.

### *The role of replication in strengthening confidence in effects*

When a result is found to be significant there is always *some* chance that a type I error has been made. This is in the nature of statistical significance testing. We can never rule out a 'fluke' result. This is why we talk of *supporting* rather than *proving* hypotheses. However, our confidence that a real effect exists is very much strengthened by *replication*. If a difference is found to be significant with $p < 0.05$ and then a second researcher obtains significance with $p < 0.05$ using much the same design and variables, then probability tells us that this is a *very* highly unlikely outcome if no real effect exists. The most convincing effects in the research literature are those that have been replicated several times, those that are therefore *highly reliable*.

### *Different significance levels*

$p < 0.05$   This is the conventional 'milestone level' of significance. You would need a difference or correlation to be significant at this level if you wished to publish your results. A type I error may still have occurred, but replication, as we have just seen, should increase confidence in the apparent effect.

$p < 0.01$   Researchers feel more confident that they have demonstrated an effect if the probability of their result under $H_0$ is less than 0.01 (also known as the 1 per cent significance level). In cases where the result is likely to be controversial researchers would probably not submit a paper for publication unless this level was achieved. This is because they would like to be very sure that they were not making a type I error. Also, where there is no chance to go back and replicate a study (for instance, a study based on behaviour at the turn of the millennium), it would be safer to obtain results that are highly significant. In the case of research with possible human applications (such as the beneficial effects of certain drugs on brain or behaviour) researchers would probably wish to be even more certain and obtain significance with $p < 0.001$, perhaps.

**$p < 0.1$** Researchers rarely publish results where a difference has been found 'significant' with p only less than 0.1. Conventionally researchers feel this gives too much probability to the likelihood of a type I error. However, 'significance' at this level almost certainly will be a spur to further research. If a result 'just fails to make it', one can't help but feel that with a few more participants or a slightly improved design or materials, conventional significance at a 5 per cent level would be achieved.

Using levels of 0.01 or lower will have the effect of increasing the likelihood of a type II error. We may retain the null hypothesis when, in fact, there is a real difference in the underlying population.

# Tests of significant difference for measured variables.

In the explanation of significance above we found a significant difference between the two groups of values in Table 5.1. We mentioned the Mann–Whitney test as being appropriate and that if we carried it out using a computer we would obtain the exact probability of our result occurring under $H_0$. But, all we *need* to know is whether this probability passes the critical point of being less than 0.05. Simple statistical tests will tell us this without needing to resort to computers and expensive software. Next we find out how simple tests can be carried out by hand.

# Difference tests at ordinal level

## The Mann–Whitney U test
### When do I use the Mann–Whitney?

When you:

● have data at least at **ordinal level** (can be reduced from interval or ratio)

● are testing sample differences from an **unrelated design**

**The rationale** of the Mann–Whitney was given above in our explanation of significance. The test is based on the likelihood of obtaining the smaller sum of ranks, or less, given that the null hypothesis is true.

### Calculation of the Mann–Whitney U test

To carry out the Mann–Whitney test by hand on the data in Table 5.1 we proceed as follows.

| *Procedure* | *Calculation on our data* |
|---|---|
| **1** Rank all the values in the two groups (A and B) as one set; if there are many tied scores, use the formula for 'when $N$ is large' on p.115. Find the total of ranks in each group. Where appropriate, call the total for the smaller group $R_A$ and that for the larger group $R_B$ | See columns c and d, Table 5.2 Call the 'light' condition A and the 'serious' condition B <br><br> $R_A = 17 \quad R_B = 38$ <br><br> (both groups are the same size so the naming of totals is arbitrary here) |
| **2** Use the following formula to calculate $U_A$: <br><br> $U_A = N_A N_B + \dfrac{N_A(N_A + 1)}{2} - R_A$ | $U_A = 5 \times 5 + \dfrac{5 \times (5 + 1)}{2} - 17$ |

| where $N_A$ is the number of values in group A and $N_B$ is the number in group B | $= 25 + \dfrac{30}{2} - 17 = 25 + 15 - 17$ |
|---|---|
| | $= 23$ |

**3** Then calculate $U_B$ from:

$$U_B = N_A N_B + \frac{N_B(N_B + 1)}{2} - R_B \qquad U_B = 5 \times 5 + \frac{5 \times (5 + 1)}{2} - 38$$

$$= 25 + \frac{30}{2} - 38 = 25 + 15 - 38$$

$$= 2$$

| **4** Select the smaller of $U_A$ and $U_B$ and call it $U$ | Since $2 < 23$ then $U = 2$ |
|---|---|
| **5** Check the value of $U$ against critical values in Table 3 Appendix 2, taking into account $N$ in each group ($N_1$ and $N_2$ – it doesn't matter which is which). Check whether test is one- or two-tailed. | Our two sample sizes are 5 and 5. For $p < 0.05$ the $U$ has to be equal to, or less than, 2 (two-tailed). Our value *is* 2 so we have met the critical value. |
| **6** Make a statement of significance | The result is significant with $p < 0.05$. We may reject $H_0$ and conclude that we have a real effect and *not* a selection of two samples under the null hypothesis. |

# General procedure with statistical tests of significance

Earlier we outlined the thinking behind the declaration that a difference between two sets of scores is *significant*. This has been covered in some detail to show that the decision to call a difference significant is not magical or one based on intuition, 'hunch' or a simple impression of size. Once the concept of significance is properly understood, we need only choose an appropriate test and proceed with a test calculation and significance decision, as was done in the Mann–Whitney example above.

### Steps in coming to a significance decision
When testing your data for significance you should always go through the following steps:

1 **Choose an appropriate statistical test**
   Your data and your design must be appropriate for the test used. If you use Table 5.9 on page 142 you should be able to decide which test is most appropriate for your particular hypothesis.

2 **Calculate a test statistic**
   There is always a symbol (e.g. '$U$') associated with each test. For this we always calculate a particular value known as a test 'statistic'. For instance, in the Mann-Whitney test we calculated the value of $U$ as 2.

3 **Compare value of test statistic with appropriate critical value found in tables**
   For $N_1$ = 5 and $N_2$ = 5, the critical value of $U$ for $p < 0.05$ (two-tailed) was 2 and our calculated value was not greater than this. Note: for some tests the criterion is for the calculated test statistic to be *greater than* the critical value.

4 **Draw significance conclusion**
   We met the criterion that $U$ must be ≤ the critical value. Our difference is significant with $p < 0.05$. Therefore we may reject the null hypothesis.

## The Wilcoxon matched pairs signed ranks test
### When do I use the Wilcoxon?

When you:

- have data at least at **ordinal level** (can be reduced from interval or ratio);
- are testing sample differences from a **related design**.

Imagine that ten clients seen by a clinical psychologist have been undergoing a new form of therapy focused on improving self-esteem ratings. The ratings for self-esteem have been taken before and after a period of three months' therapy. The second set of ratings are taken by assistants unaware of the client's initial rating – see Table 5.4. (The attentive reader will have noticed that a much better design here would be to compare the group's change with that of a control group not receiving the new approach, but let's suppose this is all that could be managed under the circumstances.)

**Table 5.4** *Self-esteem ratings before and after three months' therapy*

| a | b | c | d | e | f |
|---|---|---|---|---|---|
| Client | Self-image rating | | Difference (c − b) | Rank of difference | Sign of difference |
| | Before therapy | After 3 months' therapy | | | |
| A | 3 | 9 | 6 | 7.5 | + |
| B | 12 | 18 | 6 | 7.5 | + |
| C | 9 | 7 | −2 | 3 | − |
| D | 7 | 7 | 0 | | |
| E | 8 | 7 | −1 | 1.5 | − |
| F | 1 | 4 | 3 | 4.5 | + |
| G | 15 | 16 | 1 | 1.5 | + |
| H | 9 | 12 | 3 | 4.5 | + |
| I | 11 | 15 | 4 | 6 | + |
| J | 10 | 17 | 7 | 9 | + |

**The rationale** of the Wilcoxon here is that if the therapy is completely ineffective, that is, if the null hypothesis is true, we would expect the differences in Column d of Table 5.4 to range randomly around zero. That being the case, the total ranks of positive and negative differences should be about equal, most of the time. If we want to show that the therapy is effective we would want the ranks of *negative* differences to be as small as possible. Negative differences are those where the outcome 'went the wrong way', where clients *worsened* in self-esteem. One or two moderate differences in the wrong direction, or a few small ones, will perhaps still leave most of the overall difference in the right direction.

## Calculation of Wilcoxon's T for related pairs of data

| Procedure | Calculation using data from table 5.4 |
|---|---|
| 1 Calculate the difference between the pairs of scores (in columns b and c), always subtracting in the same direction. | See Table 5.4 column d |
| 2 Rank the differences. Ignore the sign of the difference. Also ignore any zero values – these results are omitted from the analysis. | See Table 5.4 column e |
| 3 Find the sum of the ranks of positive differences, and the sum of ranks of negative differences. The *smaller* of these is *T*. If the sum of one set of ranks is obviously smaller, you need only add these. | Sum of ranks of *negative* signed differences (cases c and e with –2 and –1) will obviously be smaller. Therefore add their ranks: 3 + 1.5. Hence *T* = 4.5 |
| 4 Find relevant line (using *N* which does not include zero differences) in Table 2 Appendix 2 and decide whether to use one- or two-tailed values. | Relevant line is *N* = 9 (case D has been dropped). Conservatively stick to a two-tailed test. |
| 5 For significance, *T* must be *less than or equal* to a table value. Find the lowest critical value which *T* does not exceed. | *T* is less than the table value of 5 in the *p* < 0.05 column, two-tailed. |
| 6 Make a statement of significance. | The difference is significant (*p* < 0.05) Reject the null hypothesis. |

### When N is large

Rank tests use tables in which $N$ only goes up to a modest value of 20 or 25. For larger values there is a formula which produces a z-value. For significance with $p < 0.05$, z must be greater than 1.96 (2-tailed) or 1.65 (1-tailed).

The relevant formulae are:

### Mann–Whitney

$$z = \frac{U - \frac{N_A N_B}{2}}{\sqrt{\left(\left[\frac{N_A N_B}{N(N-1)}\right] \times \left[\frac{N^3 - N}{12} - \Sigma T\right]\right)}}$$

where $N$ = the sum of $N_A$ and $N_B$ and

$$T = \frac{t^3 - t}{12}$$

$T$ is calculated for *each set* of tied values and $t$ is the number of values for each tie.

### Wilcoxon signed ranks

$$z = \frac{N(N+1) - 4T}{\sqrt{\left(\frac{2N(N+1)(2N+1)}{3}\right)}}$$

where $T$ is Wilcoxon's $T$ calculated in the normal way.

## Difference tests at interval level – the $t$ tests

### When do I use the $t$ test?

When you:

- have data at interval or **ratio level**
- are testing differences between samples (**related** or **unrelated** – see below)
- have samples drawn from a normally distributed population[1]

- have sample variances which are not too different (in an unrelated design where sample sizes are noticeably different)[2.]

The tests which follow (and Pearson's correlation to be encountered further on) are often known as 'parametric' tests. This is because their calculation involves some estimation of the statistical values in the populations from which the samples have been drawn. (Don't forget these populations aren't necessarily people. It is easier to think of them as infinite populations of *scores*.) Basically the tests estimate the mean and standard deviation of the underlying *distribution* of scores so many people call them *distribution dependent* tests. All you need to recognise is that, if you are *sure* your data are at interval level (e.g. not where you have asked participants to estimate attraction on an invented 1 to 10 scale; OK where you have measures of time or number of words recalled out of a list of say 30 words) then you can use the more 'powerful' *t* test, *so long as*, the other criteria above (normal distribution and homogeneity of variance) are also met.

## If you have a related design – the related *t* test

**The rationale** for the related *t* is similar to that for the Wilcoxon. Let's suppose that the 'self-image' ratings taken in Table 5.4 were actually produced by a well standardised and professionally recognised test. In these circumstances many researchers would claim

[1] (from previous page) This is usually very difficult to establish. You can: 1. argue that this should be so (since other researchers have used a *t* test on the same sort of data); 2. inspect your sample data if the samples are large enough (say 2 × 30) to see if the shape of the distribution takes on a roughly normal distribution shape; 3. reject the *t* test, reduce data to ordinal level and conduct the appropriate rank difference test above.

[2] This is known as the *homogeneity of variance* criterion. If you are using a related design, or an unrelated design where sample sizes are equal or very nearly so, then ignore it. If not and the variances look very different you can: 1. check in a programme like SPSS to see if they are significantly different and follow SPSS instructions; 2. reject the *t* test, reduce data to ordinal level and conduct the appropriate rank difference test above.

that the data could be treated as *interval level* data (but this *does* remain a strong debate). In that case we would again expect, under the null hypothesis, all the differences to range around a mid-point of zero. In this case we stick with that point, we *don't* reduce the data to ranks, and we see whether the mean of the differences is a good deal *above* zero; far enough above to say that, *if the null hypothesis is true*, we wouldn't expect that kind of mean difference very often in a set of randomly picked differences from a population centring around zero.

Let's proceed then to test these two paired sets of data using the related *t* test.

### *Calculation of related* t *test for a set of data pairs*

| Procedure | Calculation on our data | |
|---|---|---|
| Find the *variance* of the set of *differences* between the pairs of data (see column d of table 5.4) which we will call $s_d^2$. The procedure for calculating variance was given in Chapter 4 (p.82). Remember that the formula is: $$s^2 = \frac{\Sigma(x - \bar{x})^2}{n - 1}$$ only in this case we are finding the variance of the *differences* in column d as if these were a set of scores (in the equation above substitute *d* for *x*). Hence we have to find the *mean of the differences* and use this to calculate $s_d^2$ for the differences (d). If you have the right sort of calculator you can find the mean and variance of the 10 differences in a jiffy; if not calculate as opposite: | Differences: 6, 6, –2, 0, –1, 3, 1, 3, 4, 7 Mean of differences: 2.7 (=$\bar{d}$) Deviations of differences from mean: | |
| | $d - \bar{d}$ | $(d - \bar{d})^2$ |
| | 6 – 2.7 = 3.3 | 10.89 |
| | 6 – 2.7 = 3.3 | 10.89 |
| | –2– 2.7 = –4.7 | 22.09 |
| | 0 – 2.7 = –2.7 | 7.29 |
| | –1– 2.7 = –3.7 | 13.69 |
| | 3 – 2.7 = 0.3 | 0.09 |
| | 1 – 2.7 = –1.7 | 2.89 |
| | 3 – 2.7 = 0.3 | 0.09 |
| | 4– 2.7 = 1.3 | 1.69 |
| | 7 – 2.7 = 4.3 | 18.49 |
| | $\Sigma d = 27$ | |
| | $\Sigma(d - \bar{d})^2$ | = 88.1 |
| | $\dfrac{\Sigma(d - \bar{d})^2}{N - 1} = \dfrac{88.1}{9} = 9.79$ | |
| | $s_d^2 = 9.79$ | |

**Then we use the formula:**

$$t = \frac{\bar{d}}{\sqrt{(S_d^2/N)}}$$

$$t = \frac{2.7}{\sqrt{(9.79/10)}} = 2.73$$

Compare *t* with the critical value found in Table 5, Appendix 2, for the appropriate *degrees of freedom*. Don't worry about these. They have to do with how many pairs of scores you have. They are calculated, *for a related t*, as *N* – 1 when *N* refers to the number of paired values in your set.

$df = 10 - 1 = 9$

Critical value for p < 0.05, df = 9, 2 -tailed = 2.26

Our value for *t* needs to be *higher* than this for a significant result. It *is*, so we can reject our null hypothesis at the 5% level (*p* < 0.05).

There is another version of the formula for related *t* if you cannot easily calculate the variance of a set of values. It is:

$$t = \frac{\Sigma d}{\sqrt{\left(\dfrac{N\Sigma d^2 - (\Sigma d)^2}{N-1}\right)}}$$

Here we would enter the value of $\Sigma d = 27$, the value for $\Sigma d^2$ $(6^2 + 6^2 + -2^2 + 0^2 + -1^2 + 3^2 + 1^2 + 3^2 + 4^2 + 7^2) = 161$ and the value for $(\Sigma d)^2 = 27^2 = 729$.

Be careful not to confuse $(\Sigma d)^2$ and $\Sigma d^2$!

Try this calculation and you should get the same result as we got for the other version of the related *t* test – 2.73.

## If you have an unrelated design – the independent (or unrelated) *t* test

Let's assume we have taken a sample of extrovert and introvert students and counted the number of compact music discs on their shelves under the hypothesis that extroverts get bored with music more quickly and will therefore buy discs more frequently. As before, you must realise that we would not usually work with such small samples but the data in Table 5.5 will suffice to demonstrate how to calculate the independent *t* test. Table 5.5 shows that the extrovert mean (13.2) is indeed greater than the introvert mean (9.2) but is this difference a wide enough one to count as significant?

**The rationale** for the independent *t* test is that the difference *between* means must somehow be compared with the variation *within* the groups. To demonstrate that this must be so, consider this. If your class gained an average of 60% in an end of term test and another class gained 57%, although your group might crow about 'winning' you would know that the difference was not really a significant one if there was a wide variation within your group and within theirs (people scoring from 20% right up to 85%, for instance). However, if the variation was *narrow* (their maximum was 61% and minimum 55%) it might look as though your group were *generally* better overall.

For the unrelated *t* test I'm afraid there's no easy route and we have a rather nasty looking formula to contend with:

$$t = \frac{\overline{x}_a - \overline{x}_b}{\sqrt{\left[\frac{\left(\Sigma x_a^2 - \frac{(\Sigma x_a)^2}{N_a}\right) + \left(\Sigma x_b^2 - \frac{(\Sigma x_b)^2}{N_b}\right)}{(N_a + N_b - 2)}\right]\left[\frac{N_a + N_b}{(N_a)(N_b)}\right]}}$$

Although this is nasty let's just take a closer look at it. The expression on top is simply the difference *between* the two means. This is what we wish to test to see whether they are significantly different. The expression on the bottom is something like the average standard deviation *within* the two groups. Hence here we *are* comparing the difference *between* means (on top) with the variation *within* the groups (underneath), as was briefly explained above. If the variation is *small*, relative to the difference *between* means, *t* will be large. When it's large enough we will find a significant difference. So let's get to work:

**Table 5.5** *Number of music CDs in students' rooms*

| Extrovert | | | Introvert | |
|---|---|---|---|---|
| $x_a$ | $x_a^2$ | | $x_b$ | $x_b^2$ |
| 14 | 196 | | 8 | 64 |
| 9 | 81 | | 9 | 81 |
| 12 | 144 | | 5 | 25 |
| 11 | 121 | | 13 | 169 |
| 20 | 400 | | 11 | 121 |
| $\Sigma x_a =$ 66 | | $\Sigma x_b =$ 46 | | |
| $\bar{x}_a =$ 13.2 | $\Sigma x_a^2 =$ 942 | | $\bar{x}_b =$ 9.2 | $\Sigma x_b^2 =$ 460 |

## Calculation of independent t test for two unrelated sets of data

| Procedure | Calculation on our data |
|---|---|
| **1 Find:** $\Sigma x_a$ | 66   See Table 5.5 |
| $(\Sigma x_a)^2$ | $66^2 = 4356$ |
| $\Sigma x_a^2$ | 942   See Table 5.5 |
| **Be careful to distinguish between these last two terms** | |
| **2 Find** $(\Sigma x_a)^2/N$ | $= \dfrac{4356}{5} = 871.2$ |
| **3 Find** $\Sigma x_a^2 - (\Sigma x_a)^2/N$ | $= 942 - 871.2 = 70.8$ |
| **4 Find:** $\Sigma x_b$ | 46   See Table 5.5 |
| $(\Sigma x_b)^2$ | $46^2 = 2116$ |
| $\Sigma x_b^2$ | 460   See Table 5.5 |
| **5 Find** $(\Sigma x_b)^2/N$ | $= \dfrac{2116}{5} = 423.2$ |
| **6 Find** $\Sigma x_b^2 - (\Sigma x_b)^2/N$ | $= 460 - 423.2 = 36.8$ |
| **7 Add the results of steps 3 and 6** | $70.8 + 36.8 = 107.6$ |
| **8 Divide the result of step 7 by** $N_a + N_b - 2$ | $\dfrac{107.6}{(5 + 5 - 2)} = \dfrac{107.6}{8}$ $= 13.45$ |

| | | |
|---|---|---|
| **9** Multiply the result of step 8 by $\dfrac{N_a + N_b}{N_a \times N_b}$ | $13.45 \times \dfrac{5+5}{5 \times 5} = 13.45 \times 0.4$ | |
| | $= 5.38$ | |
| **10** Find the square root of step 9 | $\sqrt{5.38} = 2.32$ | |
| **11** Divide the difference between the two means ($\bar{x}_a - \bar{x}_b$) by the result of step 10 For an unrelated $t$ test $df = N - 2$ | $\dfrac{(13.2 - 9.2)}{2.32} = \dfrac{4}{2.32}$ $t = 1.72$ $df = 10 - 2 = 8$ | |

| | |
|---|---|
| Consult Table 5 in appendix 2 to find what critical value our calculated value of $t$ 'beats' | Our obtained value of $t$ (1.72) does not exceed the critical value in the table where $t$ must be greater than 2.3 (two-tailed) or 1.86 (one-tailed) for $p < 0.05$ |

We did not find a significant difference between the two means and must retain the null hypothesis that extroverts and introverts do not differ on number of CDs possessed in their rooms.

# Tests of significant difference for categorical variables

## Difference tests at nominal level

### The (binomial) Sign Test
### When do I use the Sign test?

When you:

- have data at **nominal level** (can be reduced from interval or ordinal)
- are testing sample differences from a **related design**.

We can use the sign test on the same data in Table 5.4 on which we earlier calculated Wilcoxon's $T$. We can use the data in column f where we only pay attention to whether a client has improved or not. We could have used the actual scores as we did in the Wilcoxon example. However, one can imagine studies in which *all* we know for each client is whether they improved or not. This would make the variable *categorical* rather than measured (just a '+' or a '–').

**The rationale** for the sign test is really the first part of the argument for the Wilcoxon. If there really is no improvement caused by the therapy then we should expect column f of Table 5.4 to contain a roughly equal number of positive and negative signs. This is what the null hypothesis predicts here. We want to show that the *actual* number of negative signs obtained was highly unlikely ($p < 0.05$) if this null hypothesis is true. For the Table 5.4 therapy example this probability is exactly the same as that for drawing 9 socks from a drawer containing equal numbers of black and white socks and finding that no more than two socks are white.

## Calculation of the Sign test

| Procedure | Calculation on our data |
|---|---|
| 1 Calculate the difference between the pairs of scores (in columns b and c), always subtracting in the same direction. | See Table 5.4 column d |
| 2 Record the direction of each difference as positive or negative. Ignore any zero values – these results are omitted from the analysis. | See Table 5.4 column e Ignore case D |
| 3 Find the frequency of the signs which occur less often. Call this value $S$ | Negative signs are less frequent. There are two of these (cases C and E). Hence $S = 2$ |
| 4 Find the relevant line (using $N$ which doesn't include zero differences) in Table 1 (Appendix 2) and decide whether to use one – or two-tailed values. | Relevant line is $N = 9$ (case D has been dropped). Conservatively stick to a two-tailed test. |

| 5 For significance, $S$ must be *less than or equal* to a table value. Find lowest critical value which $S$ does not exceed. | $S$ is greater than the table value of 1 in the $p < 0.05$ column, two-tailed. |
|---|---|
| 6 Make statement of significance. | Difference is not significant ($p > 0.05$). Retain the null hypothesis. |

You might find it odd that using the sign test gives us a non-significant result whereas the Wilcoxon gave us a significant one. However, this is solely because the sign test is far cruder. It ignores the *size* of differences and uses *only* their direction. We are working with nominal rather than ordinal level data. Important information has been lost and, because we don't (perhaps can't in other cases) employ a more sensitive test, we are missing an important effect. We will probably make a type II error if we use the sign test here rather than the Wilcoxon.

## The chi-square ($\chi^2$) test
### When do I use the chi-square test?

When you:

- have data at **nominal level** (can be reduced from interval or ordinal)
- are testing differences between sample frequencies from an **unrelated design** (or an association between sample frequencies).

The chi-square test assesses differences between the ratios of sets of frequencies though it is often called a 'test of association' because it *also* tells you whether being in one category of one variable (e.g. 'opposed to animal testing') is *associated* with being a member of a category on another variable (e.g. 'student').

### A simple chi-square test – are students opposed to animal testing?

Suppose your work group decides to conduct a small-scale survey on attitudes to animals. As part of the questionnaire you ask students the following question:

**'Are you opposed to the testing of animals in the making of cosmetic products?' Yes/No**

Your group asks students selected at random from your course. Let us suppose that you find the following frequencies occur:

**Observed frequencies**
For animal testing      15 (a)    Against animal testing      25 (b)

**Expected frequencies**
You were hoping to show that students are generally against animal testing so a relevant null hypothesis here is that any difference we have found is solely the result of sampling bias from a population with equal numbers of people who are pro- and anti-animal testing. This is what we would like to reject if we wish to support the proposition that a *majority* are *against* testing. When we conduct a significance test we assume the null hypothesis is true. If it is true here, we would expect, from 40 respondents, to find 20 *for* testing and 20 *against*. This is what would be most likely to occur if we simply asked each person to toss a coin. We say that our *expected frequencies* are 20 in each cell (a and b). Note that the expected frequencies are what we expect *if the null hypothesis is true*. They are *not* what we actually expect to happen.

**Rationale for the chi-square test:** The chi-square test is appropriate here because we have a *categorical* (or '*nominal*') variable. The response to the animal testing question can only be 'yes' or 'no'. We do not have a measured score for each participant and we are dealing with overall *frequencies* – how many said 'yes' and how many said 'no'. We want to investigate the difference between these two totals and the frequencies are *unrelated* – the people saying 'yes' are different from all the people saying 'no'.

## Calculation on the sample data (single variable chi-square test)

The formula for all chi-square calculations is:

$$\chi^2 = \sum \frac{(O-E)^2}{E}$$

1  So as not to get confused, give each 'cell' of the data table a letter – this has been done for the observed frequencies above, using 'a' and 'b'.

2  Calculate the *expected frequencies*. These are the frequencies we would expect *under the null hypothesis*. To calculate expected frequencies in this kind of simple (single variable) chi-square test, where the null hypothesis assumes equal frequencies in each cell, just divide the total frequencies by the number of cells. We have a total of 40 spread across two cells. Hence our expected frequency table is:

Expected frequencies:
For animal testing      20 (a)     Against animal testing      20 (b)

3  Refer to observed frequencies as 'O' and to expected frequencies as 'E'.
For each cell, following the $\chi^2$ formula above, calculate steps I) to V) as follows:

| I | II<br>$O - E$ | III<br>$(O - E)^2$ | IV<br>$(O - E)^2/E$ | V<br>Total of column IV results |
|---|---|---|---|---|
| Cell a: | $15 - 20 = -5$ | $-5^2 = 25$ | $25/20 = 1.25$ | |
| Cell b: | $25 - 20 = 5$ | $5^2 = 25$ | $25/20 = 1.25$ | |
| | | | | $\chi^2 = 2.5$ |

4  Our value for $\chi^2$ is 2.5. This has now to be checked against tables of critical values to see whether our $\chi^2$ is large enough to enable us to reject the null hypothesis. The critical value from tables will be the value of $\chi^2$ which would occur 5% of the time or less *if the null hypothesis is true*. To check the critical value we need to calculate our *degrees of freedom*.

5 Degrees of freedom, written as *df*, are based on the number of cells (*k*) in our frequency table. In general for a single variable chi-square, *df* = *k* – 1, so here, with two cells we have
*df* = 2 – 1 = 1
6 Find the appropriate critical value for $\chi^2$ by consulting Table 4 Appendix 2, and using *df* = 1, two-tailed test with *p* = 0.05. The critical value is 3.84
7 Our value for $\chi^2$ was 2.5 and the critical value to beat is 3.84. (Note that in chi-square tests our calculated value for chi-square must *exceed* the critical value). This means that our value has failed to reach the critical level and we must *retain the null hypothesis* that pro and anti testers are equally represented among students.

### *A more complex chi-square test – are students more opposed to animal testing than non-students?*

Disheartened by this result it strikes you that the null hypothesis here assumed a 50:50 split of opinion in the general population. Your result for 40 students did not differ far enough from this 50:50 ratio for you to be able to claim significance. What might be of interest would be to compare students, not with a *hypothetical* baseline but with the *actual* population of non-students. Imagine that your colleagues decide to compare 40 students with 40 people of roughly the same age, education and cultural background but who are *not* students. Now we might obtain the following data:

**Table 5.6** *Observed (fictitious) frequencies of students and non-students opposed to, and in favour of, animal testing*

|  | Position on animal testing | | |
|---|---|---|---|
|  | for | against | total |
| Students | 14 (cell a) | 26 (cell b) | 40 |
| Non-students | 24 (cell c) | 16 (cell d) | 40 |
| Total | 38 | 42 | 80 |

The data above are formed into what is known as a *2 × 2 frequency table*. Our rationale for what is now a 2 × 2 chi-square test is the same as before. However, this time we are testing the difference between frequency distributions for two samples – those for the students and those for the non-students.

## Calculation on the sample data (2 × 2 chi-square test)

1 As before, to avoid confusion, label the cells. This time we have a to d

2 Calculate expected frequencies. This time we base the null hypothesis on the *overall* totals in Table 5.6. If there were equal numbers of students and non-students (which there were) and there is no difference between the populations (this is the basis of the null hypothesis) then the 38 who were for testing should be equally split between student and non-student. The general formula for calculating expected frequencies in this sort of table is:

$E = R \times C/T$

where $R$ is the total of the row the cell is in, $C$ is the column total for the cell and $T$ is the overall frequency total. Calculating here we get:

Cell a  $38 \times 40/80 = 19$
Cell b  $42 \times 40/80 = 21$
Cell c  $38 \times 40/80 = 19$
Cell d  $42 \times 40/80 = 21$
to give the table:

| | Position on animal testing | | |
|---|---|---|---|
| | for | against | total |
| Students | 19 (cell a) | 21 (cell b) | 40 |
| Non-students | 19 (cell c) | 21 (cell d) | 40 |
| Total | 38 | 42 | 80 |

3 Applying the formula and calculating as before we get:

| I | II | III | IV | V |
|---|---|---|---|---|
| | O – E | $(O - E)^2$ | $(O - E)^2/E$ | Total of column IV results |
| Cell a: | $14 - 19 = -5$ | $-5^2 = 25$ | $25/19 = 1.32$ | 1.32 |
| Cell b: | $26 - 21 = 5$ | $5^2 = 25$ | $25/21 = 1.19$ | 1.19 |
| Cell c: | $24 - 19 = 5$ | $5^2 = 25$ | $25/19 = 1.32$ | 1.32 |
| Cell d: | $16 - 21 = -5$ | $-5^2 = 25$ | $25/21 = 1.19$ | 1.19 |
| | | | $\chi^2 = 5.02$ | |

4  Our chi-square value is 5.02. Now we need to calculate *df*.

5  The general formula for calculating *df* in a frequency table with multiple rows and columns is:

$df = (R - 1)(C - 1)$

where *R* is the number of rows and *C* is the number of columns. So here *df* are:

$(2 - 1) \times (2 - 1) = 1$

6  Consulting Table 4 again for *df* = 1, *p* = 0.05, two-tailed* we find the critical value is again 3.84.

7  This time our calculated value is greater than the critical value, so we can claim significance and reject the null hypothesis. We say that there is a significant difference between the frequency proportions for students and non-students ($p < 0.05$). Put another way, we can claim support for an association between being a student and being opposed to animal testing.

## *Limitations on the use of chi-square*

- Chi-square can only be used on *frequencies*. It cannot be used where the numbers in each cell represent proportions, ratios, percentages etc.

- The frequencies in each cell must be entirely *independent*. A person cannot appear in more than one cell. This would happen, for instance, if we compared the responses of biology

---

*You should always consult two-tailed values when using chi-square except in the special case of the one variable only test where there are just two categories – as in the first example on students and animal testing. In that special case the same reasoning for one tailed tests applies as was described on page 106

and psychology students on animal testing and found that several students in our sample were taking both subjects.

- Statisticians used to argue that having any expected frequencies lower than five markedly increased the chance of a type I error. Nowadays this rule is relatively relaxed but it is still a good rule of thumb. If you get expected frequencies as low as this in two or three cells of a $2 \times 2$ design, you should consider adding more data or changing the design in some way. Chi-square results are relatively secure if the total sample size is well above 20.

- Like correlations (see below) chi-square demonstrates a relationship between variables. It cannot in any way lead to a conclusion that one variable was the cause of the other. This interpretation depends upon whether the design was strictly experimental or not.

## Correlation

Figure 5.4 shows in fairly dramatic style the way in which two variables can be closely *related* . We can see from this chart that as unemployment increases so burglaries increase. However, as we just said above for chi-square, what we may *not* conclude from the chart, no matter how tempting the theory, is that unemployment *causes* burglary to increase. The data do not show this. They *support* this view but there are many other possible interpretations.

Correlation concerns *relationships* between sets of values, rather than the *differences* between their central tendencies or frequencies which we have considered so far. Instead of asking what is the difference between ice cream sales for a cold month and a warm month, we ask 'to what extent do ice cream sales vary throughout the year as the temperature varies? What else tends to increase as the temperature rises towards Summer? We can think of plenty and these could include: sales of sun cream, losses of temper, boiling car radiators, the length of metal bridges and so on.

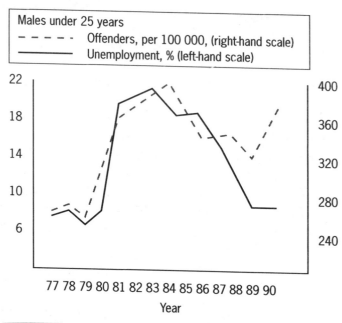

**Figure 5.4** *Burglary and unemployment rates by year*

Correlation between two variables then refers to:

'the extent to which scores on one variable tend to change consistently with changes in score on another variable'.

What sorts of correlations might we expect to find in the study of psychology? Here are a few possible relationships:

- verbal memory and verbal reasoning;
- hand reaction time and foot reaction time;
- level of stress experienced and symptoms of psychological disorder;
- level of self-esteem and level of motivation to achieve.

In Chapter 2 we said we might compare the average number of hours of sleep students had per night over a year with their final exam grades. Suppose we obtained the (fictitious) results shown in Table 5.7.

**Table 5.7** *Average hours sleep (for a year) and exam grades*

| Participant | Average hours' sleep per night | Exam grade | Rank of hours' sleep | Rank of exam grade | Difference d | d² |
|---|---|---|---|---|---|---|
| 1 | 8.5 | 63 | 10 | 6 | 4 | 16 |
| 2 | 5.8 | 52 | 2 | 3 | –1 | 1 |
| 3 | 5 | 35 | 1 | 1 | 0 | 0 |
| 4 | 6.1 | 45 | 3 | 2 | 1 | 1 |
| 5 | 7.2 | 58 | 6 | 5 | 1 | 1 |
| 6 | 7.4 | 64 | 7.5 | 7 | 0.5 | 0.25 |
| 7 | 6.9 | 70 | 5 | 9 | –4 | 16 |
| 8 | 7.4 | 65 | 7.5 | 8 | –0.5 | 0.25 |
| 9 | 6.6 | 56 | 4 | 4 | 0 | 0 |
| 10 | 7.5 | 71 | 9 | 10 | –1 | 1 |
| | | | | | $\Sigma d^2$ = | 36.5 |

## Calculation of correlation

The pairs of scores in Table 5.7 seem quite closely related. That is, where a participant has little sleep they also tend to have a low exam grade. We can see this easily by looking at the *rank* of the scores in columns 4 and 5. For instance, participant number 3 is ranked 1 on sleep and 1 on exam grade; the equivalent ranks for participant 4 are 3 and 2.

The *degree* of correlation can be assessed by calculating a *correlation coefficient*. This is a number between −1 and +1 which represents the *strength* of a correlation between two variables. In the case of temperature and ice cream sales we would expect a close positive relationship and a figure of perhaps 0.8, this being fairly close to +1. If two variables are not at all related we expect a value around zero (0).

### Negative correlation

What would be happening if a correlation coefficient turned out to have a value between −1 and 0? Such a correlation is known as a *negative correlation*. Just think what tends to *decrease* as average sleep increases? Perhaps the more students sleep the less they drink alcohol, given that they have less time in which to do any drinking! If we took measures of sleep and alcohol consumption we might find a correlation of, say, –0.75. In a negative correlation, as values on one variable increase the values on the other decrease.

## Finding a specific value for the correlation coefficient

We can only calculate this sort of correlation relationship if both variables are *measured* – see page 73. This means that for each variable each person must have an individual *score* or at least a rank. We cannot correlate, for instance:

- marital status (single, married etc.) and wealth;
- political party a person votes for and their annual salary;
- attitude to corporal punishment and daily newspaper preferred.

As an exercise, in each of the examples above pick the variable which, as it stands, makes the use of a correlation impossible (answers in footnote*).

## Spearman's rho (ρ) – a correlation for ordinal level

### When do I use Spearman's rho?

When you:

- have data at **ordinal level**
- are testing pairs of scores for a **correlation**.

The symbol for Spearman's correlation coefficient is ρ. This is spelt 'rho' and pronounced 'ro'. In the formula though we can use $r_s$

$$r_s = 1 - \frac{6 \times \Sigma d^2}{N(N^2 - 1)}$$

---

*Marital status; political party; preferred newspaper. In each case, these are *categorical variables* – we cannot give people a *score* on these variables. There is no numerical value that puts them *between* one person and another.

**Rationale for Spearman's rho:** the Spearman formula should not be too intimidating. $N$ is the number of pairs of values you have (usually the number of participants, so 10 in our example) and the only other value which can vary is $\Sigma d^2$. Let us see why we look at this value. In Table 5.7 you can see that column 6 is the *difference* between each person's rank on sleep and exam grade. If there is a strong correlation between these two variables what should the differences between ranks be? Well, with a strong correlation people should rank about the same on one variable as they do on the other. Therefore the *differences* between ranks should be small or, ideally, zero. If you look at the formula for rho given above, if all the differences are small then $\Sigma d^2$ will be small, the top of the equation will be small and the whole fraction similarly small. Hence, we will have little to subtract from 1 and should end up with a strong correlation (near to 1). Let us step through the calculations now:

### *Calculation of Spearman's ρ on sleep and exam grade data*

| Procedure | Calculation using data from Table 5.7 |
|---|---|
| 1  Give ranks to values of $x$. | See column 4 of Table 5.7 |
| 2  Give ranks to values of $y$. | See column 5 of Table 5.7 |
| 3  Subtract each rank for $y$ from each rank for $x$. | See column 6 of Table 5.7 |
| 4  Square results of step 3. | See column 7 of Table 5.7 |
| 5  Add the results of step 4. | Total of column 7 = 36.5 |
| 6  Insert the result of step 5 into the formula for $r_s$ above where $N$ is the number of pairs. | $r_s = 1 - \dfrac{6 \times 36.5}{10(10^2 - 1)}$ $= 1 - \dfrac{219}{990} = 1 - 0.221$ $r_s = 0.779$ |

## Interpreting the correlation coefficient – the strength and significance of correlations

What we discover from this calculation is that our value for correlation is 0.779. This is quite a *strong* value, since it is fairly close to +1. However, we do not automatically know that it is a *significant* value. The argument for significance is much the same as we have already encountered:

- assume the null hypothesis $(H_0)$ that the population correlation is zero
- find the probability that our degree of correlation would occur if $H_0$ is true
- dismiss $H_0$ if this probability is lower than 0.05.

### Checking the significance of our correlation

| Procedure | Calculation using data from Table 5.7 |
|---|---|
| Consult Table 6 in Appendix 2. Our value of $r$ has to be equal to or greater than the table value for significance Make significance statement. | Critical value for $p < 0.05$, where $N = 10$ and test is two-tailed is 0.648. Our result, 0.779, is greater than this critical value. Correlation is significant so reject $H_0$. |

If you inspect Table 6 Appendix 2 you can see that *strong correlations are not always significant.*

Where we only have a small number of paired values the correlation has to be very high indeed before we can call it significant. On the other hand, if we have a large number of values a quite small correlation can be significant. With $N = 40$ even a correlation of around 0.3 can be significant and this is what leads to the statement often made about survey results that there was a '... weak but significant trend' shown in the data'.

## Pearson's $r$ – a correlation for interval level
### When do I use Pearson's $r$?

When you:

- have data at **interval** or **ratio level**
- are testing pairs of scores for a **correlation**
- have samples drawn from a normally distributed population*

Equation for Pearson's correlation:

$$r = \frac{\Sigma(x - \overline{x})(y - \overline{y})}{(N - 1)s_x s_y} \qquad (1)$$

this converts to a nastier looking form:

$$r = \frac{N\Sigma xy - \Sigma x \Sigma y}{\sqrt{[N\Sigma x^2 - (\Sigma x)^2][N\Sigma y^2 - (\Sigma y)^2]}} \qquad (2)$$

However we shall use equation (2) in the calculation below as this can be done without first calculating standard deviations. If your calculator or computer does standard deviations easily then equation (1) is the formula for you! Note that the standard deviations are the population estimate versions (using $N$–1).

The *rationale* for the Pearson is much the same as that for the Spearman. Here however, the calculation deals with actual score values, not their rank values. In the formula above I hope you can see that the size of the top part of equation (1) depends upon the multiplication of one's deviation on one variable with one's deviation on the other variable. If the match between pairs of scores is close then a person high on one variable will be high on the other. Therefore, their deviations will both be high and we will get a high value for the multiplication of the deviations. A symmetrical argument goes for those who are *low* on both variables. Hence, to the extent that people do tend to get a high score on one variable if they have a high score on the other, and vice versa, we will get a *higher* value on the top part of the equation.

---

* With the same reservations as for the $t$ tests – see page 116

## Worked calculation of Pearson's r on sleep and exam grade data in Table 5.8

| Procedure | Calculation on our data (equation 2) |
|---|---|
| **1** Find: $\Sigma x$ | 68.4 See Table 5.8 |
| $(\Sigma x)^2$ | $68.4^2 = 4678.56$ |
| $\Sigma x^2$ | 476.88 See Table 5.8 |
| Be careful to distinguish between these last two terms | |
| **2** Find: $\Sigma y$ | 579 See Table 5.8 |
| $(\Sigma y)^2$ | $579^2 = 335241$ |
| $\Sigma y^2$ | 34685 See Table 5.8 |
| **3** Multiply each $x$ by each $y$ to obtain $\Sigma xy$ | $= 4043.9$ See column 5 of Table 5.8 |
| **4** Multiply the result of step 3 by $N$ | $= 4043.9 \times 10 = 40439$ |
| **5** Multiply $\Sigma x$ by $\Sigma y$ | $= 68.4 \times 579 = 39603.6$ |
| **6** Subtract the result of step 5 from the result of step 4 | $= 40439 - 39603.6 = 835.4$ |
| **7** Multiply $N$ by $\Sigma x^2$ | $= 10 \times 476.88 = 4768.8$ |
| **8** Subtract $(\Sigma x)^2$ from the result of step 7 | $= 4768.8 - 4678.56 = 90.24$ |
| **9** Multiply N by $\Sigma y^2$ | $= 10 \times 34685 = 346850$ |
| **10** Subtract $(\Sigma y)^2$ from the result of step 9 | $= 346850 - 335241$ $= 11609$ |
| **11** Multiply the result of step 8 by the result of step 10 | $= 90.24 \times 11609$ $= 1047596.16$ |
| **12** Find the square root of the result of step 11 | $\sqrt{1047596.16} = 1023.52$ |
| **13** Divide the result of step 6 by the result of step 12 | $= 835.4/1023.52 = 0.816$ Pearson's $r = \mathbf{0.816}$ |
| **14** Consult Table 7 in Appendix 2, using $N-2$ $df$ and expect to 'beat' the critical value if your correlation is to be significant | Critical value of $r$ from Table 7 for $N = 8$ and p < 0.05, two-tailed, is 0.632. Our value easily beats this so we report our correlation as significant (p < 0.05). |

**Table 5.8** *Average hours sleep (for a year) and exam grades*

| Column 1 Variable *x* Average hours sleep per night | Column 2 | Column 3 Variable *y* Exam grade | Column 4 | Column 5 |
|---|---|---|---|---|
| *x* | $x^2$ | *y* | $y^2$ | $x \times y$ |
| 8.5 | 72.25 | 63 | 3969 | 535.5 |
| 5.8 | 33.64 | 52 | 2704 | 301.6 |
| 5 | 25 | 35 | 1225 | 175 |
| 6.1 | 37.21 | 45 | 2025 | 274.5 |
| 7.2 | 51.84 | 58 | 3364 | 417.6 |
| 7.4 | 54.76 | 64 | 4096 | 473.6 |
| 6.9 | 47.61 | 70 | 4900 | 483 |
| 7.4 | 54.76 | 65 | 4225 | 481 |
| 6.6 | 43.56 | 56 | 3136 | 369.6 |
| 7.5 | 56.25 | 71 | 5041 | 532.5 |
| $\Sigma x = 68.4$ | $\Sigma x^2 = 476.88$ | $\Sigma y = 579$ | $\Sigma y^2 = 34685$ | $\Sigma xy = 4043.9$ |

## Plotting correlation – the scattergram or scattergraph

We can investigate the kind of relationships that exist between variables by plotting pairs of data on what is known as a scattergram or scattergraph. Figure 5.5 shows such a plot for the sleep and grade scores given in Table 5.8. The chart is formed by plotting *one* point for each *pair* of values. Hence, participant 2's pair of scores is indicated on the chart (see the two dotted lines) by a point which represents 5.8 on the x-axis (hours of sleep) and 52 on the y-axis (exam grade).

If people tend to score high on one variable and high on the other, their scores will appear in the top right of the chart. If people score low on sleep and low on grade, their scores will appear in the bottom left hand corner. The overall effect then will be a line of points going upwards from left to right as in Figure 5.5. This is the typical shape for a positive correlation. A *negative correlation* is indicated in Figure 5.6, where fictitious scores on sleep and alcohol consumption show a distribution of paired points running top left to bottom right. Correlation scattergrams are very rarely anything like a straight line. The shapes in Figure 5.7 demonstrate the sort of shape one might expect for various values of correlation.

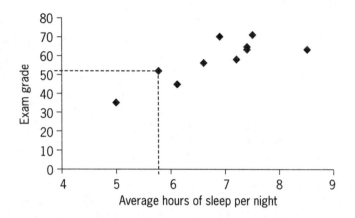

**Figure 5.5** *Correlation between hours of sleep and exam grade*

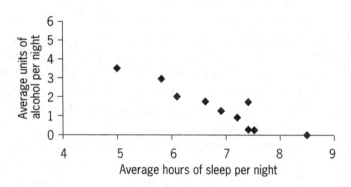

**Figure 5.6** *Correlation between hours of sleep and alcohol consumption*

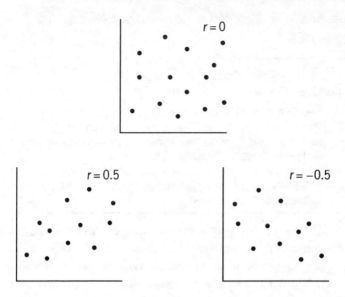

**Figure 5.7** *Scattergram shapes for different sizes of correlation*

## The temptation to assume *cause* with a correlation

We now return to a point made right at the start of the section. Remember we said that from a strong *correlation* between unemployment levels and burglary rates we may not infer a *cause and effect* relationship between these two variables. It does not show that increases in unemployment *cause* the burglary rate to rise, however tempting this *interpretation* may be. Recent research into use of the Internet (Kraut *et al.,* 1998) shows that higher levels of Internet use correlated with greater levels of depression and reported loneliness. A Guardian newspaper report drew the conclusion that use of the Internet was a *cause* of the psychological symptoms. Of course, all we can conclude is that there is *support* for this view. The correlation *equally* supports the view that people who are more depressed and lonely are more likely than others to *indulge* in use of the Internet. Typically, when a politician or media speaker believes that A causes B, and refers to a correlation as support, if we are not critical in our thinking, we are led to assume that evidence of a cause effect relationship has just been presented.

---

**PAUSE FOR THOUGHT:**

Consider the following statements:

* there is a strong correlation between the use of physical punishment by parents and later levels of aggression in the punished child; if physical punishment were not used we would see lowered levels of aggression in children.
* the number of higher education graduates correlates very well with the health of the economy; if we want a positive economy we should train more graduates.

---

In each case, the first part of the statement confirms the existence of a correlation between variable A and variable B. However, the practical suggestion in the conclusion does *not* necessarily follow at all. When faced with a correlation between two variables to interpret you should always consider in turn the three major ways of interpretation shown in Figure 5.8.

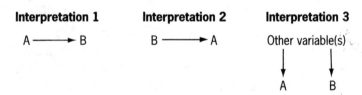

**Figure 5.8**  *Possible interpretations of a correlation*

We would need to eliminate the alternative explanation, that B may be a cause of A (perhaps aggressive children provoke the use of physical punishment; perhaps a healthier economy produces more graduates). There is also the possibility that a third factor, variable C, is a cause of similar variation in both A and B. If we put two thermometers, one Celsius and one Fahrenheit, beside each other on a table we would get a perfect correlation between the two readings but one is not the cause of the changes in the other. Both would be affected systematically by a third factor, the ambient temperature! Perhaps both aggression and physical punishment are the products of a certain type of environment. Perhaps healthy economies and greater numbers of graduates both result from periods free of war and other social disturbance. So, when asked about the interpretation of a correlation always consider these three simple relationships. More complex ones are also possible.

## Choosing an appropriate statistical test

You can use Table 5.9 to choose the appropriate significance test to use on your data, but first you need to answer the following questions in this order:

1 **Difference or correlation?**

   Are you looking for a *difference* between samples of scores or for a *correlation* between pairs of scores, one on each of two measured variables?

2 **Level of data measurement – categorical or measured?**

   For *differences*, you need to decide whether your data are *measured* or *categorical*. If they are in categorical form (frequency counts in categories) then treat them as *nominal level* data. If they are measured variables you have to decide whether to treat them as *interval* level data or whether to play safe and reduce them to *ordinal* level data (by *ranking* them).

3 **Type of design – related or unrelated data?**

   For differences you also need to decide whether the research design for these particular data is *related* or *unrelated*. Do you have two sets of data where each score in one set is paired specifically with a score in the other set? This will happen where participants have performed the same task under different conditions (repeated measures) or where matched and paired participants have each performed the same task, but in two different conditions.

**Table 5.9** *Table for choosing an appropriate significance test*

| Nature of hypothesis test: | Type of research design | |
|---|---|---|
| | unrelated | related |
| **Differences** | | |
| *Categorical variable* | | |
| Nominal level data | Chi-square | Sign test |
| *Measured variable* | | |
| Ordinal level data | Mann–Whitney | Wilcoxon (matched pairs) |
| Interval level data | Independent *t* test | Related *t* test |
| **Correlation** | | |
| Ordinal level data | | Spearman ρ |
| Interval level data | | Pearson *r* |

# Conclusions

We have seen that there is a statistical convention for deciding whether or not a difference found between two groups or conditions should be regarded as significant. This decision is based on the probability of getting a particular result (difference or correlation) if there really is no effect in the underlying population (i.e. there is really nothing 'going on'). On this basis many 'fluke' results will be accepted as representing a real effect and many differences will be thought to be random errors when there *is* a real underlying effect. However, if the convention is followed there should be a gradual accumulation of reliable effects; real effects will be replicated by other researchers, whereas 'fluke' results will not be replicated. It is the duty of psychological researchers to be honest about their data and open about their statistical testing procedures, otherwise the unwitting lay public might be exposed to apparent effects, the scientific basis of which is quite unsound (for example, differences taken seriously that are actually not significant and correlations interpreted as evidence for cause–effect relationships).

# Summary

- When a difference between two samples is tested for **significance** it is assumed that the two samples are drawn from identical populations or populations with the same mean (the **null hypothesis** $H_0$). The probability of their occurrence is then calculated if this null hypothesis is true. When this probability falls below $p = 0.05$ the difference is recognised as **significant**. The null hypothesis is then rejected and the **alternative hypothesis** (that populations, or their means, are different) is supported.

- A **non-directional hypothesis** must be tested with a **two-tailed test** – one which calculates the probability under $H_0$ of getting a difference as high as the one found in **either** direction that the difference could take. **Directional hypotheses** may be tested using a **one-tailed test** under certain restrictions but doing this in psychology can be controversial.

- A **type I error** is said to occur when the null hypothesis is rejected although in fact it is true. A **type II error** concerns retaining the null hypothesis when it is really false (i.e. failing to detect a real effect).

- Differences with $p < 0.01$ are sometimes said to be 'highly significant' and would be required where research findings are controversial, e.g. reversing the previous research trend. Differences with $p < 0.1$ are not significant but may be pointers to further, more refined research.

- Significance tests usually calculate a **test statistic** and this is checked against tables to see whether the **critical value** (for significance with $p < 0.05$) has been reached.

- The **Mann–Whitney** procedure tests differences between the ranks of two **unrelated** samples of data (ordinal level).

- The **Wilcoxon matched pairs signed ranks test** does the same for **related** data.

- The **t** tests are used on related or unrelated designs when data are at interval level and certain 'parametric assumptions' about the data are met (samples from a normal distribution; homogeneity of variance where the design is unrelated and sample sizes are quite different.)

- **Chi-square** tests the **association** between frequencies for two **categorical variables**. It can also be seen as testing the difference between two or more distributions of frequencies for categorical variables.

- The **binomial sign test assesses** significant difference between pairs of related data at the **nominal level** of measurement where only the **sign** of the difference between pairs is used.

- Chi-square will be larger, and approaches significance, as the distance between **observed** and **expected frequencies** increases, expected frequencies being those 'expected' under the null hypothesis.

- **Correlation coefficients** fall between −1 and +1 and can therefore be **positive** (one variable **increases** with the other) or **negative** (one variable **decreases** as the other **increases**).

- **Spearman's rho** assesses the strength of **correlation** between pairs of scores on two variables using the rank of each score in its set (ordinal level data).

- **Pearson's _r_** assesses the strength of a correlation between pairs of scores on two variables where scores are at an interval level of measurement.

- The **significance** of a correlation coefficient depends upon the size of the sample ($N$). Where $N$ is large a small correlation can be significant but where it is quite small a large correlation would be required for significance.

- Correlations can be plotted on a **scattergram** with different values producing typical shapes.

- Care must be taken with the interpretation of a **significant correlation**. Without further evidence, the temptation to assume that one variable is obviously the **cause** of the other needs to be critically checked. The correlation **alone** can provide no evidence of causal direction.

# THE USE AND ANALYSIS OF QUALITATIVE DATA

**6**

## Introduction

In Chapter 1 we briefly encountered the distinction between *quantitative* and *qualitative* data. Chapters 4 and 5 have been concerned entirely with the analysis and reporting of quantitative data. It is time now to look at the ways in which psychological researchers gather, analyse and report their findings when their research project has included the gathering of *qualitative* data – data which are verbal or visual meanings and not numerical.

### The distinction between qualitative data and qualitative research approaches

**Qualitative data:** these are pieces of information about the world, obtained through research, which have not been given a numerical value. If you ask someone what they think about the use of animals in psychology experiments you will hear arguments, reasons, opinions, beliefs and (perhaps emotional) attitudes. The pieces of language used to express these views are *qualitative data*. They have not been reduced to numerical values of any kind.

**Qualitative (research) approaches:** a qualitative approach is one in which there is a commitment to gather only, or mainly, qualitative data. However, there is also usually a commitment to *treat* the data as qualitative and not to turn them into numbers at some stage. Hence a qualitative report does not often contain statistical summaries and concentrates mainly on verbal description and analysis of qualitative data.

The emphasis in a qualitative approach is on obtaining information from people in as natural a manner and setting as possible. It is hoped that people will produce genuine views and opinions when permitted to respond freely and that behaviour observed in a natural, unconstrained setting will be *realistic* and *authentic*. Qualitative data are not recorded in segments or recorded and divided into categories already decided by the researchers. Behaviour and speech are treated as a whole. A complete record of behaviour or talk is obtained and analysis attempts to organise and explain these data, not by reducing to scores, but by a certain amount of categorising and a search for common 'themes' or ideas. As far as possible the original data are kept in their original form (for instance, quotations from the actual interview transcript).

**Table 6.1**   *Types of quantitative and qualitative data*

**Quantitative data**

- score on a personality test;
- time to complete a puzzle;
- number of people who cross on a red light;
- number of one word utterances.

**Qualitative data**

- transcript of interview with open questions;
- pictorial, for example graffiti;
- content of nursery rhymes and stories;
- video recordings of behaviour.

## The limitations of quantitative data

Quantitative data are numerical in form (even if they are only frequency counts). They are some form of *measure* of behaviour. Quantitative data very often represent only a very narrow window on the human behaviour they were taken from. For instance, suppose you present a questionnaire containing the following items:

a. **Animal experiments in psychology should be banned.**
b. **We can discover some things from animals that just cannot be discovered from studies on humans.**

Respondents have to answer on a scale choosing from:

| strongly agree | agree | undecided | disagree | strongly disagree |
|:---:|:---:|:---:|:---:|:---:|
| 1 | 2 | 3 | 4 | 5 |

Here, we can *only* discover where our respondents place themselves on this scale and the *only* information we shall have about their attitude at the stage of results analysis is that an individual scored 2 on item **a**, or, say, 26 points out of a possible 30 overall. We now have *quantitative* data – participants' responses in numerical form so that we can compare one respondent with another and we can look at differences between groups of people.

## Critique of quantitative data approaches

Many critics of quantitative methods argue that the comparison just described gives us only an *illusion* of scientific measurement and objectivity. Two people could differ quite markedly, and in unique ways that are of central interest to research, ways which are connected with quite different behaviour patterns, yet they may both score 3 on item **a** or 26 on the questionnaire as a whole. One person's *reasons* for agreeing that animal experiments in psychology should be banned could be extremely illuminating and quite different from another person's reasons. These different

reasons might determine quite different behaviour in relation to decisions about animal experimentation. One person with 26 might be moved to start a publicity campaign whereas another with 26 might not even contribute to that campaign. Their reasons might help us to understand and predict such differences in behaviour.

### Pre-structured or flexible?

In a questionnaire approach then, because it is already *structured* before we start data collection, we are limited to obtaining information *only* from items in the questionnaire and *only* in the form determined by the response system ('strongly agree'... etc.). In an experiment, we can only use the measures of the dependent variable that have been taken (response time, number of errors made, etc.). However, in a *qualitative* approach it is usually possible to gather 'open-ended' data from respondents, data which are not already forced into categories and numbered, losing their original richness. In addition, many qualitative projects permit the *addition* of questions and strategies *as the project progresses* so that insights and issues which *emerge* during the research can be incorporated into the data gathering period and used to strengthen the eventual findings.

### The strengths of quantitative data

The reason why quantitative approaches and measurement have been so popular in psychology is that these approaches, used in the physical sciences at least, have led to great success in theory development and further knowledge of how the world works. It is often *necessary* to use some form of quantitative data when attempting to check out the following sorts of claim:

- normal people would not agree with silly answers just because other people do
- most four-year-olds cannot select a different perspective from their own
- bi-lingual children perform worse in school

- women have weaker mathematical skills than men
- the 'race' of a person does not affect people's assessment of their ('aggressive') behaviour

In *all* the cases above we need at least to count and compare numbers in order to dispute the 'common sense' view. In all the cases above strong quantitative evidence exists to show that the claims are quite wrong. For instance, at GCSE level mathematics since at least 1994, girls have performed at the same level as boys and sometimes better. In other words, we *need* numbers to show that 'armchair' claims about human behaviour are *wrong*. Quantitative data make this kind of comparison possible.

**Table 6.2** *Strengths and weaknesses of qualitative and quantitative data*

| Data type | Strengths | Weaknesses |
|---|---|---|
| **Qualitative** | Original richness of data is retained Behaviour and speech should be more realistic and genuine. | Harder to compare different studies and analyses Weaker check on reliability of observers. |
| **Quantitative** | Can directly check 'armchair' claims about human differences Can use strong, established statistical theory to test significance Can publicly check and agree analysis. | Numbers give false 'scientific' image but reduce original rich information to a misleading unit Interesting hypotheses are made very narrow by the need to operationalise variables. Need for standardisation creates an artificial testing environment and a 'distant' researcher |
| | Can check reliability of observers. | Predetermined structure of measurement is imposed on participants. |
| | Bias is eliminated through large samples and standardised training. | Elimination of bias is largely the responsibility of individual researchers and their personal attempt to stay 'objective'. |

A quantitative approach also improves the possibility of *replication* of studies to obtain the same kinds of results. The *reliability* of observers and interviewers is relatively simple to check using quantitative comparisons, for instance by *correlating* their ratings of the same behaviour. Because data are directly comparable it is also possible to *publicly check* and agree upon the results of any analysis. This is not at all as easy in the case of qualitative data analysis where any two researchers could emerge with varying interpretations of what has been seen or said.

Although qualitative data have a better 'feel' to them for many psychologists (because they are the 'real' unadulterated products of people), they too have their problems in being used as evidence in psychological theory. Suppose a researcher conducts a participant observation study on an organisation using open-ended interviews with workers, asking them about their attitudes towards management, communication within the company and how satisfied they are with their jobs. The researcher also observes people working and attends meetings, taking field notes. How do we know that a different researcher would obtain just the same sort of information? How does the researcher decide what to report out of the mass of information that is available? One researcher might organise the information quite differently from another and might see quite different events or the same events quite differently. These are problems of objectivity, reliability and validity.

## Content analysis

Let us look at a method of gathering and dealing with qualitative data which is not far removed from the quantitative type of approach. Originally, *content analysis* was devised for sampling and analysing messages from the media and other recorded material, such as literature, politicians' speeches, or wartime propaganda. Attempts to analyse media messages can be dated back to the turn of the twentieth century, when various writers were concerned about the influence of the press on society, crime and morals. Before and during the Second World War content analysis was used to analyse politicians' speeches and propaganda messages.

Nowadays content analysis is used for a wide range of research purposes and these can be roughly grouped under three headings as follows.

**Analysis of existing and naturally produced data e.g.:**

- media advertisements
- news stories
- television drama
- plays
- graffiti
- legends
- suicide notes
- textbooks
- publicity campaigns
- children's' stories
- popular music
- political posters

**Analysis of participants' accounts of natural events e.g.:**

- diary records (e.g. student learning activities, new mothers' experiences)
- accounts of traumatic events
- dream reports
- interviews (e.g. with women on their experiences as political leaders)

**Analysis of artificially produced material from research e.g.:**

- responses to pictorial material (e.g. Rorschach ink blot)
- essays
- children's discussions of maths problems

## How is content analysis done?

In 'classic' content analysis, materials are coded using a predetermined coding system that has been established prior to the main research, using sample materials. Hence, coders know what categories to look for, exactly which events to record and which to ignore. This version is therefore very much like a structured observation study and is not one of the stronger 'qualitative approaches' described above. Its value is that at least it admits purely qualitative data to the spectrum of psychological research but these data are still dealt with in a fairly conventional, quantitative manner, once coded into categories.

An example of this kind of approach is the work of Cumberbatch *et al.* (1990), who analysed over 500 prime-time advertisements sampled from two weeks of television in 1990. All the advertisements were taped so there was plenty of time and flexibility for researchers to decide what to code and what not to include in the data recording process. However, the main coding work was carried out by three assistants who were trained to a point of almost perfect *reliability* in their codings (see page 59). Once trained using a sample, they used a very comprehensive coding system to classify the content of all the rest of the material.

Some of the findings were that: 75 per cent of men but only 25 per cent of women were judged to be over 30 years old. Men outnumbered women two to one. Eighty nine per cent of voice-overs, especially for expert/official information, were male. Fifty per cent of female voice-overs were categorised as 'sexy/sensuous'. The ratio of women to men rated as 'attractive' was three to two. Men were as likely to be engaged in housework for friends as for their family, whilst females predominantly worked for their family and never for friends.

## The process of content analysis

**Sampling:** depending on the research aims and interest, the researcher has to decide which materials to sample from the population as a whole. If we are interested in printed media portrayals of women, shall we sample broadsheet as well as tabloid newspapers, if so, which ones and when? Shall we include special interest magazines (e.g. gardening), local papers, supplements, travel brochures and so on? In the case of television we might hypothesise that drama programmes portray intact families (non-divorced parents) more frequently than the actual proportion in our society. To carry out such an investigation we would need to specify which sorts of drama were to be examined. If we include soaps as well as one–off dramas we would need to sample according to the relative frequency on television of each type of drama. We would also need to sample proportionately from different channels, times of day, serious and light drama and so on.

**Coding units:** we must decide which aspects of content we are going to include and how we are going to code them. For instance, suppose we were looking only at portrayal of women and men in newspaper advertisements. We might decide that one coding unit is to be that of 'caring for others', with a possible prediction that women will be scored more frequently on this category than men. Each person appearing in an advertisement would be coded '1' if their role can be classed as caring (e.g. cooking for family member, helping another) and '0' if not. Another example might be a rating of 1 to 5 on the degree of 'control of the situation' an advertisement character is seen to exert.

---

**PAUSE FOR THOUGHT**

Try to think of other categories of role or behaviour on which women and men in newspaper advertisements might be coded. (Examples in the footnote*)

---

## Procedure

In a typical study, a sample of material is analysed closely by the researchers and a coding scheme developed. Assistants are then trained and asked to use the coding system on the main collection of materials. To avoid researcher bias, assistants coding the main body of data may be completely unaware of ('blind to') the research hypothesis or aim. The codes or ratings given by the assistants can be correlated to assess inter-coder or inter-observer reliability.

| Activity | | Group members | | Role | |
|---|---|---|---|---|---|
| At work | 1 | Alone | 1 | Subordinate role | 1 |
| At home | 2 | With one person, opposite sex | 2 | Dominant role | 2 |
| Leisure activity | 3 | With one person, same sex | 3 | Equal status role | 3 |
| Sporting activity | 4 | With several people, same sex | 4 | No obvious role | 4 |
| Travelling | 5 | With several people, opposite sex | 5 | | |
| Other | 6 | With mixed sex group | 6 | | |

### *Analysis*

From the examples just given it should be clear that in this approach, although data are originally in qualitative form, they are *converted* to quantitative data in the form of codes or ratings. Once in this form regular significance tests can be performed, for example on the difference between male and female ratings or frequencies for control or caring.

# Qualitative research with qualitative analysis

When a *qualitative approach* is taken, rather than just the analysis of qualitative data, the usual assumption is that statistical summary and significance testing will *not* be the focus of attention and will usually be absent. Rather, data are reported in qualitative form where the emphasis is on meanings that have emerged or experiences that have been recorded.

There is no one way to analyse qualitative data in a qualitative manner; there are several (sometimes competing) qualitative research approaches, each with a somewhat different outlook on the philosophy of truth, science and social science research. In the space available I can only outline a few general principles, give guidance on some commonly used techniques, and direct you towards more substantial and varied resources.

# Doing qualitative research

The data gathering *methods* used in a qualitative research investigation may well be several of those mentioned earlier, such as semi-structured interviewing, participant observation and so on. The *content* could be stories, speech, drawings, graffiti and so on. Questions which it will certainly help to answer before setting out on a qualitative project are: 'What is the major *purpose* of this project? What will it attempt to achieve? How far will it go?' This is similar to thinking about the structure of measures and related data-testing issues before starting to gather quantitative data.

## Aims in qualitative research

Qualitative studies, like quantitative studies, can have various overall aims. Working with qualitative data gathered on observed behaviour or reported experiences, three major categories of aim are:

- attempts to describe and explore the data;
- hypothesis testing using the data;
- attempts to generate theories from the data.

These aims may overlap in any one study. Some qualitative approaches involve theory generation *during* the gathering of data and a return for more data, based on the themes and categories that have so far emerged from the analysis. Theory *generation* is really quite a sophisticated level of qualitative research and will not be discussed further here (but see Coolican, 1999), or several of the qualitative research references (see last section in this chapter), especially Richardson, 1996 and Hayes, 1997. Pidgeon & Henwood (1997) recommend that new students in psychology might usefully limit themselves to the *taxonomy development* (i.e. categorising) stage of qualitative analysis using a grounded theory approach. *Grounded theory* makes no prior assumptions about what will be found among qualitative data and it does not usually set out to test a hypothesis or confirm a theory. It involves searching the qualitative data set for themes and categories in order to eventually develop new theories.

## Describing and exploring qualitative data

It is possible to use qualitative data to start investigating an area or simply to record and assess the experiences of a particular group or individual. Such a study could be an exploration of students' attitudes to study after the end of formal education. It could be self-identification issues for British-born teenagers whose parents were immigrants. It could ask people to recall their reactions to the sudden death of Princess Diana in 1997 and their response to the special atmosphere this created.

There are several issues and problems that arise from such studies and these are particularly important for the student on an introductory psychology course who would like to conduct a qualitative research study as part of their coursework requirement.

### How will the final report differ from journalism?

An acceptable report of psychological research must differ from what might be found in a popular magazine article. It must avoid conclusions based on subjective perceptions of events and personal anecdotes, though these may appear as part of the researcher's reflections in some part of the report.

Examination boards and tutors often warn against reports of the 'day at the zoo' or 'observation of my cute baby brother' variety. It is important to distinguish between a *social* or *personal* problem and a *psychological research problem*. Hence, psychology coursework reports that are 'an account of my friend's battle with anorexia' or 'bullying at a secondary school' can be fascinating but may lack any reference to psychological issues, constructs, processes or relevant theory. What should be identified before starting the project is a psychological research question and the approach used in trying to answer it must also be *psychological*.

### What is the perspective of the researcher?

Any two people observing the behaviour of just one child will invariably come up with differing accounts of the child's actions. If the topic is aggression one can imagine the conversation:

'Oh, that was vindictive'.
'Oh, I don't know. The other little girl provoked her and it wasn't such a hard pinch.'

In quantitative approaches we saw that raters are trained to use a strict coding system and this has the strength of producing observer reliability but the disadvantage of inflexibility. In qualitative approaches the emphasis is generally on the richness of data and the complete picture. This immediately introduces the problem of the observer's own perspective and attitudes. Qualitative approaches mostly accept that there is no one 'truth' to be observed. They recognise that what we perceive is a *construction*. It is hard simply to observe a 'hit'. What we perceive is an action in a context. Facts do *not* 'speak for themselves'. We instantly incorporate any raw data 'facts' through our existing set of attitudes, prejudices, preferences, biases and so on.

Hence it is important that throughout a qualitative research project the writer keeps in mind the fact that they are perceiving data through their own perspective and that there could be other ways of interpreting what is recorded and indeed that another observer might have chosen to record different events. This is something like the quantitative researcher saying that although a significant difference occurred there are several possible explanations of that difference other than the one proposed in the research study.

### What to do then? Searching for categories and themes

At the very least, the qualitative researcher must categorise data. The set of data will need order imposing upon it. It has to be organised so that comparisons and contrasts can be made. Each category or theme which the researcher suggests will need to be exemplified with direct samples from the data, often being samples of the exact speech produced, for instance, in open-ended interviews. The aim of qualitative analysis, however, is not to count *occurrences*, though this is not ruled out. The aim is more to use occurrences as *examples* and to reflect the *variety* of participant perspectives among the entire data set.

## A practical example

Suppose we were investigating the explanations students give for coming to study at Learnwell College. We may start with sheets of actual statements made by participants, either in interviews or on questionnaire returns.

The first step is to read through the entire set of statements perhaps several times. No doubt, even before reading through once, there will be certain types of statement that we have already noticed many times such as 'to help me get a decent job' or 'because I really couldn't find anything else I fancied'. We already have the tentative categories of *future job* and *best option*. Reading through all the statements will help to confirm this pattern and to identify further categories and themes.

### Emerging categories and themes

A *category* tends to be a fairly clear 'bin' to collect all similar statements, for instance, all those that indicate that a reason for coming to the college was to get a qualification to help in getting a better job than would otherwise have been possible. A *theme* tends to emerge either from the joining of several categories or from a more general notion that cuts across several categories. For instance, students might often refer, rather negatively, to the college course being not what they would *really* like to do (the best options being unrealistic or unattainable), not what they would have chosen if they had the money. The theme might therefore be termed 'best of a bad lot' and cut across 'best option', 'only option' and even 'future job' (where, for instance, there were better but more costly routes to a chosen career).

### Coding

The next job is to *code* each statement according to the category or theme it represents. A statement can fall into several categories or themes. A traditional method of coding has been to take several (photo)copies of each statement and place each physically into category or theme *files*, using a cross-reference system to record multiple filings. Nowadays there are several computer programmes that will do this job (see Coolican, 1999; Grbich, 1999, or contact CTI Psychology, Department of Psychology,

University of York, York YO1 5DD, or their Internet site at http://www.york.ac.uk/inst/ctipsych/web/CTI/DirTxt/reviews/r contents.html). It is also relatively simple to use a regular word processor or spreadsheet to organise and sort statements.

## Recording the categorisation process

It is important at this stage that the researcher does not get 'carried away' by apparent insights and great discoveries about categories and themes. Qualitative approaches tend to emphasise a flexible and fluid process of category development. As further data are analysed or as data are revisited several times, it will inevitably occur that categories need to be revised. The researcher should keep a cool perspective and constantly review the organisation so far devised. The researcher can record this process of category development and the changes that occur along with the reasoning that prompted the changes. It is even possible to go out and gather more data to 'fill out' relatively empty categories or to establish that further categories might emerge when more appropriate or more complete questions are asked or when different people, or more of one type, are asked.

## The 'fit' of the data to categories

The student researcher might also start to explain how well all the data 'fit' the categories and themes that have been developed. They can note the fuller categories and those that are more tentative or relatively empty. They might even postulate that opposite categories might emerge if further data were gathered, or if different people were asked, recognising that this is now impossible given the project schedule and deadline. They can try to identify obvious deficiencies and perhaps begin to develop tentative links between some of the categories.

Most important of all is to note where certain statements simply fail to fit any of the categories at all. In this case either these are noted as odd, or else categories are altered or developed until such statements *do* fit somewhere.

### Developing hypotheses

During analysis, especially as links are developed, it may well be that hypotheses emerge that are suitable for quantitative testing, either now or as the subject of a possible future and more specific research study. It might be, for instance, that we note that older students tend to mention more often that they chose to study *mainly* because they are interested in learning for its own sake – they just love academic study. This can be tested quantitatively, either through the *content analysis* route described above, using the existing data, or by devising a new, more strictly defined and operationalised study, using say a structured questionnaire and an eventual significance test on the mean scores of different age groups.

### Individual cases

Having developed a set of categories the researcher might closely analyse the statements of just one individual ('one case') and look for contrasts or inconsistencies. Variation in what people say about the same thing need not be seen as 'error' but as an indication that the issue is complex and that each individual can respond from several perspectives at different times or following different sorts of question. Variation can also be used to demonstrate the different actions people perform with speech in conversations – an approach used in *discourse analysis* in particular. People can be seen as *constructing* their views with speech rather than simply *reporting* them – for instance: 'Oh I don't know, perhaps I really *did* come here more for the music, men, fun and not so much for the hands-on advantage of BTEC.'

### Memo-writing

The term 'memo-writing' (see Charmaz, 1995, for a full description) refers to the writing of explanations as the descriptive process progresses. Memos can be produced as footnotes or even physical 'post-It' notes attached to different files and statements. What they explain can be:

- the justification for a separate category or theme;
- why certain statements are allocated to categories;
- why one category is linked to another;
- why a theme is linked to or across categories;
- why a further category might emerge with further data collection;
- why one individual's statements are seen as contradictory;
- how various categories or themes may be linked to previous theory.

### Relationship to theory

Even 'purely descriptive' work can be related at some point to existing theory. Children's sayings can be related to Piaget's cognitive stages or to his themes of animism or concepts of justice. A good example of a qualitative and exploratory article (Kerwin et al., 1993) generated many hypotheses and challenged a background of theoretical assumptions. Counsellors and social workers had often simply assumed (from older theories) that 'biracial' children (those with parents from two different ethnicities) *must* have problems with self-esteem, cultural identity, marginality and conflict. Kerwin showed that those she interviewed had far more positive ideas about their double culture and appeared to demonstrate little problematic experience at all. The article is worth obtaining for the student wishing to conduct a modest qualitative project but there is also a synopsis of the article in Coolican (1999).

## Qualitative research reports

A qualitative research report can follow much the same *overall* structure as the 'conventional' model (see page 169.) Up to the results section the only differences might be that:

- quantitative hypotheses may be replaced by qualitative ones or by specific *aims* for the research;
- the writer might give an explanation (in the introduction and/or design section) of why a qualitative approach was

thought appropriate for this piece of research and perhaps a justification for the particular qualitative approach chosen.

## The results section

If a mixed approach (quantitative *and* qualitative) is used, statistical information may be included here – for instance, tables of frequencies of occurrence of different themes or categories for different groups – but this is not essential (unless your examination board or tutor demands it). There will usually be no significance testing, though there *can* be with some forms of content analysis.

Because categories are going to be discussed and justified, as well as including actual quotations from participants, it usually makes sense for the results and discussion sections to merge. In our college study example, for instance, we might start with a description of the categories that have emerged along with any earlier version if the reasons for discarding or changing these are considered important for an understanding of the final structure. These categories might then be illuminated by typical comments taken directly from participants' speech. After each description there may be a discussion of the sorts of reasons covered by the category and of any links it might have to other categories. For any of these, a basic quantitative frequency count might well be included. Finally, we might tentatively begin to suggest which types of people might be more likely to make statements falling into particular categories (for instance, we might outline the findings on part-time evening students at this point).

As with quantitative reports, the discussion section also contains a critique of the design and method and any suggestions for further research.

## Keeping away from journalism

Whatever happens, and as mentioned above, the report *must* keep daylight between itself and popular magazine or letter writing. It is important that the writer keeps in mind at all times questions such as:

So what does this tell me about psychology?
What psychology is relevant to what I'm reporting here?
How can I relate these findings to existing psychological theories and research?
In what ways does this differ from the findings in previous research?

An account of a four-year-old's responses to questions like 'Why is a bell alive?' may be hilarious, but a psychological report needs to link these answers to psychological constructs such as animism, or an existing theory concerning the association between thinking and language.

## Reporting data objectively

One difference between journalism and psychology reporting is that the journalist has no responsibility to report *everything* that occurred. They can, especially in a feature article, report just what they need to paint the picture they wish to transmit. Researchers, however, have a responsibility not to distort data and to report everything of relevance, especially if some data do not neatly fit the theory that is being investigated.

Fielding & Fielding (1986) warn against two possible temptations:

- selecting data to fit an 'ideal conception';
- selecting data which are 'conspicuous because they are exotic'.

## Quotations

The report will usually include verbatim quotations from participants which bring the reader into the reality of the situation studied. The quotations are selected from the raw data and tend to 'tell it like it is'; they are often striking and are chosen to *exemplify* a particular view. For example:

'Life is not a dress rehearsal you know.'

Where participants' speech is *summarised*, it is important that these summaries are clearly identified as such. In the best research, and where time permits, participants are asked if they wish to read the summary in order to see that it fairly represents the sense of what they originally said and meant.

# Reliability and validity in qualitative research

Rather than using the terms *reliability* and *validity* qualitative researchers often use the terms:

- rigour
- good practice
- research evaluation.

Remember that qualitative research studies often involve long periods of interviewing and observation (sometimes with the researcher living or working with the observed group for many months or even years); the following checks on the trustworthiness of researchers' data, findings and interpretations are recommended by several writers:

- Make all field notes and transcriptions publicly available for inspection so that other researchers can come to their own conclusions about the findings (Bryman, 1988).
- Check inter-observer reliability where several assistants, for instance, are using a previously developed coding scheme to categorise qualitative findings.
- Check the fit of data to categories or theory (see above and Pidgeon & Henwood, 1997). *All* the data should fit into categories and themes *or* there should be some discussion in the report of the data which do not fit.
- *Respondent validation* is an attempt to check out findings with the original participants. For instance, summaries of what we *think* people have said can be checked with the people who said them to see that we have a fair and accurate account of their meaning.
- Keep a log or 'reflexive journal' (Lincoln & Guba, 1985) which records all problems, ideas at various stages of the

research, one's own reactions and values and their possible influence on the progress of the research. This is sometimes known as *reflexivity* – the practice of reflecting upon the ways in which the research progress may be influenced by one's own attitudes and personal insights. Such reflexivity enables other readers to see what led to certain conclusions and to suggest alternative interpretations.

- *Triangulation* – in some studies we can check what people say in an interview with the way in which they have answered a questionnaire. In navigation, triangulation is the use of two independent bearings to determine the exact position of a vessel. However, in qualitative research, triangulation might well throw up a *difference* between two methods. Interviews might produce information *contrary* to what people might have said in a questionnaire. This in itself is interesting and throws light on the contexts in which people will say one thing rather than another. Used in this sense, then, triangulation refers to trying to get more than one perspective on the same situation, events or person.

- *Repetition* – this is in some ways similar to the notion of *replication* in quantitative research. Repetition has to do with the way in which researchers first develop terms and theories from their initial data analysis, then return to the research setting (e.g. an industrial organisation) in order to gather fresh data using questions prompted by the early hypotheses. The process might occur several times.

## Conclusions

Qualitative approaches have always existed within psychological research but they have very recently become increasingly popular and will certainly continue to grow within psychology in the early years of the twenty-first century. There need be no clash between qualitative and quantitative approaches, but at present there often is. The two approaches are not irreconcilable for most researchers, but for a few there appears to be a battle which only one side can win. It certainly *is* important that psychological research expands to recognise the value and role of qualitative data. It suffered a long while under a harsh quantitative paradigm which aped 'natural science' in an exaggerated quantitative fashion. The natural sciences themselves have always encompassed some forms of qualitative approach. An emphasis on quantification has led to some fairly sterile areas of psychological research and to the public misconception that psychologists use their measuring 'instruments' to assess people's characteristics as accurately as we might measure up for a new kitchen unit! This is certainly not the case and some would argue that it never could be.

## Summary

- Distinctions were made between **qualitative data** and **qualitative approaches** and between **qualitative** and **quantitative** data, the latter having been much criticised in recent years for producing minimal information about people and an illusion of scientific reliability and validity. Quantitative data lose much of the richness and individuality contained in qualitative information about people.

- A traditional method for dealing with qualitative data has been that of **content analysis**, where a systematic and piloted **coding system** is applied to the data (typically participants' stories or media reports) and analysis takes the form of tabled frequencies and significance tests on these.

- Purely **qualitative research approaches**, however, often have aims rather than specific hypotheses to test, and the goal is often **theory production**. A good qualitative research report must however be psychological, academic and different from a media report. It also needs to take account of the researcher's own view or position since the final 'result' will be a particular arrangement of all the qualitative data, among many possible arrangements, and the interpretation of themes may be a unique construction embedded in the researcher's own perspective.

- A very common approach to qualitative analysis is that of **grounded theory** and students at an early stage of psychological study could use a part of this in developing **categories** and **themes** from their gathered qualitative data.

- The student would need to code all data, make some record of the categorisation process (e.g. by writing **memos** and/or keeping a **reflexive log**) and investigate the fit of all data to the theme and category system which emerges.

- From the above process tentative hypotheses can be developed.

- An investigation can be made into **individual cases**, looking for contrasts in the data.

- Emerging themes and categories can be linked to existing theory.

- Reports may merge results and discussion sections. They will usually contain several illuminative direct quotations and should justify the use of method and the academic objectivity of the findings and their interpretation.

- **Reliability** and **validity** in qualitative research have often been reinterpreted as **rigour**, **good practice** and **research evaluation**.

- **Respondent evaluation** involves checking out interpretations with original respondents.

- **Triangulation** involves comparing several perspectives on one phenomenon.

- **Repetition** involves returning to original sources for more data to check out emergent themes.

# Further reading and assistance for Chapter 6

BANISTER, P., BURMAN, E., PARKER, I., TAYLOR, M. & TINDALL, C. (1994) *Qualitative Methods in Psychology*. Buckingham: Open University.
A broad practical perspective on qualitative methods.

BRYMAN & BURGESS (eds) (1994) *Analysing Qualitative Data*. London: Routledge.
A useful practical volume.

EDWARDS, D. & POTTER, J. (1992) *Discursive Psychology*. London: Sage.
About the discourse approach in psychology; highly specialist and a unique approach.

FLICK, U. (1998) *An Introduction to Qualitative Research*. London: Sage.
A friendly new general guide, fairly practical in approach. Interesting to have a German perspective and one emanating from health and nursing. Nevertheless, very useful for the prospective qualitative researcher, and written at an accessible level.

HAYES (1997) *Doing Qualitative Analysis in Psychology*. Hove: Psychology Press.
This is an extremely useful text, with several 'how to' and hands on chapters. It has contributions from mainstream qualitative writers and examples of the more central contemporary approaches (including thematic analysis, grounded theory, case studies and discourse analysis) which students would be able to tackle in fairly early projects.

HENWOOD, K. I. & PIDGEON, N. F.(1992) Qualitative research and psychological theorising. *British Journal of Psychology*, 83, 97–111.
A very useful and seminal article.

MASON (1996) *Qualitative Researching*. London: Sage.
A useful, committed qualitative 'how-to book'.

*The Psychologist* (1995) – A special issue on qualitative methods, 1995, 8(3),115–8.

RICHARDSON J.P.E. (1996) (Ed) *Handbook of Qualitative Research Methods for Psychology and the Social Sciences*. Leicester: BPS Books.
A fairly recent set of edited chapters covering the qualitative–quantitative debate, and the critique of mainstream, 'old paradigm' research methods, written mainly by UK-based authors.

ROBSON (1993) *Real World Research*. Oxford: Blackwell.
Covers well what its title suggests. Describes methods for field research and includes coverage of the more mainstream qualitative methods used in contemporary social and applied psychological research, along with conventional research designs.

SMITH, J.A., HARRÉ, R. & VAN LANGENHOVE, L. (EDS) (1995) *Rethinking Methods in Psychology*. London: Sage.
Now a classic in its statements on the new approaches to research within psychology. By the same authors: see *Rethinking Psychology*, 1995, Sage.

STRAUSS, A.L. & CORBIN, J. (1990) *Basics of Qualitative Research: Grounded Theory Procedures and Techniques*. Newbury Park, CA: Sage.
Sociologically based but a useful, hands-on introduction.

# THE ELEMENTS OF A RESEARCH REPORT

A research report tells the reader everything they need to know about the research study and it does this in a logical order. You will find that reports run as follows:

- title and abstract
- introduction and hypotheses
- method
- results
- discussion
- references

with appendices where necessary to round the whole report off. The sections above tell the reader: *why* we did what we did (the rationale for our hypotheses), *how* we did our research (method), *what* we found (results), and a discussion of findings in the light of what we set out to show or test. **The following are notes, *all* of which are important and, if followed carefully, will improve your marks for practical reports**.

### Title
Simply state the independent variable–dependent variable effect (or correlation) you are looking for, e.g. 'The effect of hot and cold weather on the likelihood of giving money to a street beggar'.

### Abstract
In fewer than 150–200 words, perhaps only 6 sentences, give the main features of the study, including the *hypotheses tested, overall design, main findings* and *conclusions for theory*.

### Introduction
Write no more than a couple of sides about the background theory that leads into the rationale for your study. Don't write, say, three sides on unrelated memory theory because your study is about some aspect of memory. Stick close to your hypothesis and

make sure you *do* provide a rationale for, and introduce, *this particular study.*

### Hypotheses

These can only be in the most specific form, following your introduction. e.g. 'Participants will recall more words in the memory training condition than in the control condition', *not* the aim: 'Participants will memorise better after training'.

### Method

This is usually divided into the four following sub-sections:

- **Design** – the skeleton of the research. Is it experimental (give type of design) or non-experimental (give main approach – observational, interview, questionnaire, correlational, case study etc.)? Operationally define *all* variables. Give independent and dependent variables where relevant. If correlational, state exactly the variables involved. State variables and design for *each* hypothesis.
- **Participants** – not just how many and the sex breakdown but also, where from exactly? How were they recruited? What selection procedures were used?
- **Materials** – not a list! Describe in sentences what was used on/with the participants but not necessarily the computer software used in the analysis of results. State how observations are coded or questionnaires are scored (here if not in the early part of the results section).
- **Procedure** – the exact steps taken with each (group of) participants and in the piloting of any materials (e.g. questionnaire). *Not* the obvious fact that 'results were collected and analysed'.

### Results

Start with a description in words (text) of your main findings (means of groups, standard deviations, etc. – whichever is most appropriate). *Support this* with a table which has a clear heading and labels for columns and rows. It must *stand alone* so the reader can tell what the values in it are measures or summaries of. A chart (known as a 'figure') can also support the data here but do not litter your report with them. You will not gain any extra marks – one chart is usually enough. Do not draw a 'bar chart' with a column representing each participant's individual score. Do not include tables of raw scores (i.e. one or two scores for each participant). All data presented must be a *summary only* of values found.

Don't define for the reader what a mean or standard deviation *is* (or how a Mann–Whitney test works). Assume they are familiar with basic statistical tools.

Follow the description with an analysis. This is very often the testing of two groups' scores (e.g. their means) for a significant difference. Often it is, instead, a correlation. Always state *exactly* what is being tested. Never say 'the results were tested'; say instead, for instance, 'the means of errors made in the alone and audience conditions were tested for significant difference ...'. State *which* test is being used and *why* (e.g. level of data measurement, type of test [differences], type of design [related/unrelated]). State the test result (e.g. value of Mann–Whitney $U$). Then immediately state the level of probability for this statistic to occur under the null hypothesis (e.g. 'This is significant with $p < 0.05$). State whether one- or two-tailed, and *df* or $N$ (where appropriate). Finally state whether the null hypothesis is to be *rejected* or *retained* (not 'accepted' or 'proven' etc.).

### *Discussion*

Start by discussing the implications of your results – the theory from your introduction which is supported or challenged and in what ways and *why*. Discuss any special, unusual or marked findings. Discuss reasons why the findings may be invalid or have failed to show the expected effect. This is a critique of your design, a search for possible confounding variables or sampling errors (etc.). Discuss how far the finding might safely be generalised, given that you will usually have tested only a tiny sample of any population. Give recommendations for improving the research next time. Discuss ways in which the research could be *extended* to test more theory but *avoid* knee-jerk reactions like 'we should test more participants' or 'we should test for sex differences' unless you can provide *a good reason for doing so*. Finally, give an overall conclusion which summarises results and implications.

### References

Each named researcher you have mentioned in your text should appear in your 'reference' list. Background texts you have consulted but *not* mentioned should go in another list entitled 'background reading' or 'bibliography'. References should include *all* details, not just a repeat of the name and date! (i.e. for books: name, initials, *title*, place of publication and publisher for journal articles: name, initials, title, *journal*, **volume**, part number and pages.)

# STATISTICAL TABLES

**Table 1** *Critical values in the Binomial Sign Test*

| N | Level of significance for one-tailed test | | | | |
|---|---|---|---|---|---|
| | 0.05 | 0.025 | 0.01 | 0.005 | 0.0005 |
| | Level of significance for two-tailed test | | | | |
| | 0.10 | 0.05 | 0.02 | 0.01 | 0.001 |
| 5 | 0 | — | — | — | — |
| 6 | 0 | 0 | — | — | — |
| 7 | 0 | 0 | 0 | — | — |
| 8 | 1 | 0 | 0 | 0 | — |
| 9 | 1 | 1 | 0 | 0 | — |
| 10 | 1 | 1 | 0 | 0 | — |
| 11 | 2 | 1 | 1 | 0 | 0 |
| 12 | 2 | 2 | 1 | 1 | 0 |
| 13 | 3 | 2 | 1 | 1 | 0 |
| 14 | 3 | 2 | 2 | 1 | 0 |
| 15 | 3 | 3 | 2 | 2 | 1 |
| 16 | 4 | 3 | 2 | 2 | 1 |
| 17 | 4 | 4 | 3 | 2 | 1 |
| 18 | 5 | 4 | 3 | 3 | 1 |
| 19 | 5 | 4 | 4 | 3 | 2 |
| 20 | 5 | 5 | 4 | 3 | 2 |
| 25 | 7 | 7 | 6 | 5 | 4 |
| 30 | 10 | 9 | 8 | 7 | 5 |
| 35 | 12 | 11 | 10 | 9 | 7 |

Calculated S must be EQUAL TO or LESS THAN the table (critical) value for significance at the level shown.

SOURCE: F. Clegg, *Simple Statistics*, Cambridge University Press, 1982. With the kind permission of the author and publishers.

**Table 2** *Critical values of* T *in the Wilcoxon Signed Ranks Test*

| Sample size | Levels of significance | | | |
|---|---|---|---|---|
| | One-tailed test | | | |
| | 0.05 | 0.025 | 0.01 | 0.001 |
| | Two-tailed test | | | |
| | 0.1 | 0.05 | 0.02 | 0.002 |
| N = 5 | T ≤ 0 | | | |
| 6 | 2 | 0 | | |
| 7 | 3 | 2 | 0 | |
| 8 | 5 | 3 | 1 | |
| 9 | 8 | 5 | 3 | |
| 10 | 11 | 8 | 5 | 0 |
| 11 | 13 | 10 | 7 | 1 |
| 12 | 17 | 13 | 9 | 2 |
| 13 | 21 | 17 | 12 | 4 |
| 14 | 25 | 21 | 15 | 6 |
| 15 | 30 | 25 | 19 | 8 |
| 16 | 35 | 29 | 23 | 11 |
| 17 | 41 | 34 | 27 | 14 |
| 18 | 47 | 40 | 32 | 18 |
| 19 | 53 | 46 | 37 | 21 |
| 20 | 60 | 52 | 43 | 26 |
| 21 | 67 | 58 | 49 | 30 |
| 22 | 75 | 65 | 55 | 35 |
| 23 | 83 | 73 | 62 | 40 |
| 24 | 91 | 81 | 69 | 45 |
| 25 | 100 | 89 | 76 | 51 |
| 26 | 110 | 98 | 84 | 58 |
| 27 | 119 | 107 | 92 | 64 |
| 28 | 130 | 116 | 101 | 71 |
| 29 | 141 | 125 | 111 | 78 |
| 30 | 151 | 137 | 120 | 86 |
| 31 | 163 | 147 | 130 | 94 |
| 32 | 175 | 159 | 140 | 103 |
| 33 | 187 | 170 | 151 | 112 |

Calculated *T* must be EQUAL TO or LESS THAN the table (critical) value for significance at the level shown.

SOURCE: Adapted from R. Meddis, *Statistical Handbook for Non-Statisticians*, McGraw-Hill, London (1975), with the kind permission of the author and publishers.

**Table 3a** *Critical values of* U *for a one-tailed test at 0.025; two-tailed test at 0.05\* (Mann–Whitney)*

$n_1$

| $n_2$ | 20 | 19 | 18 | 17 | 16 | 15 | 14 | 13 | 12 | 11 | 10 | 9 | 8 | 7 | 6 | 5 | 4 | 3 | 2 | 1 |
|---|---|---|---|---|---|---|---|---|---|---|---|---|---|---|---|---|---|---|---|---|
| 1 | – | – | – | – | – | – | – | – | – | – | – | – | – | – | – | – | – | – | – | – |
| 2 | 2 | 2 | 2 | 2 | 1 | 1 | 1 | 1 | 1 | 0 | 0 | 0 | 0 | – | – | – | – | – | – | – |
| 3 | 8 | 7 | 7 | 6 | 6 | 5 | 5 | 4 | 4 | 3 | 3 | 2 | 2 | 1 | 1 | 0 | – | – | – | – |
| 4 | 13 | 13 | 12 | 11 | 11 | 10 | 9 | 8 | 7 | 6 | 5 | 4 | 4 | 3 | 2 | 1 | 0 | – | – | – |
| 5 | 20 | 19 | 18 | 17 | 15 | 14 | 13 | 12 | 11 | 9 | 8 | 7 | 6 | 5 | 3 | 2 | 1 | 0 | – | – |
| 6 | 27 | 25 | 24 | 22 | 21 | 19 | 17 | 16 | 14 | 13 | 11 | 10 | 8 | 6 | 5 | 3 | 2 | 1 | – | – |
| 7 | 34 | 32 | 30 | 28 | 26 | 24 | 22 | 20 | 18 | 16 | 14 | 12 | 10 | 8 | 6 | 5 | 3 | 1 | – | – |
| 8 | 41 | 38 | 36 | 34 | 31 | 29 | 26 | 24 | 22 | 19 | 17 | 15 | 13 | 10 | 8 | 6 | 4 | 2 | 0 | – |
| 9 | 48 | 45 | 42 | 39 | 37 | 34 | 31 | 28 | 26 | 23 | 20 | 17 | 15 | 12 | 10 | 7 | 4 | 2 | 0 | – |
| 10 | 55 | 52 | 48 | 45 | 42 | 39 | 36 | 33 | 29 | 26 | 23 | 20 | 17 | 14 | 11 | 8 | 5 | 3 | 0 | – |
| 11 | 62 | 58 | 55 | 51 | 47 | 44 | 40 | 37 | 33 | 30 | 26 | 23 | 19 | 16 | 13 | 9 | 6 | 3 | 0 | – |
| 12 | 69 | 65 | 61 | 57 | 53 | 49 | 45 | 41 | 37 | 33 | 29 | 26 | 22 | 18 | 14 | 11 | 7 | 4 | 1 | – |
| 13 | 76 | 72 | 67 | 63 | 59 | 54 | 50 | 45 | 41 | 37 | 33 | 28 | 24 | 20 | 16 | 12 | 8 | 4 | 1 | – |
| 14 | 83 | 78 | 74 | 69 | 64 | 59 | 55 | 50 | 45 | 40 | 36 | 31 | 26 | 22 | 17 | 13 | 9 | 5 | 1 | – |
| 15 | 90 | 85 | 80 | 75 | 70 | 64 | 59 | 54 | 49 | 44 | 39 | 34 | 29 | 24 | 19 | 14 | 10 | 5 | 1 | – |
| 16 | 98 | 92 | 86 | 81 | 75 | 70 | 64 | 59 | 53 | 47 | 42 | 37 | 31 | 26 | 21 | 15 | 11 | 6 | 1 | – |
| 17 | 105 | 99 | 93 | 87 | 81 | 75 | 67 | 63 | 57 | 51 | 45 | 39 | 34 | 28 | 22 | 17 | 11 | 6 | 2 | – |
| 18 | 112 | 106 | 99 | 93 | 86 | 80 | 74 | 67 | 61 | 55 | 48 | 42 | 36 | 30 | 24 | 18 | 12 | 7 | 2 | – |
| 19 | 119 | 113 | 106 | 99 | 92 | 85 | 78 | 72 | 65 | 58 | 52 | 45 | 38 | 32 | 25 | 19 | 13 | 7 | 2 | – |
| 20 | 127 | 119 | 112 | 105 | 98 | 90 | 83 | 76 | 69 | 62 | 55 | 48 | 41 | 34 | 27 | 20 | 13 | 8 | 2 | – |

\* Dashes in the body of the table indicate that no decision is possible at the stated level of significance.

For any $n_1$ and $n_2$ the observed value of *U* is significant at a given level of significance if it is *equal* to or *less* than the critical values shown.

SOURCE: R. Runyon and A. Haber (1976) *Fundamentals of Behavioural Statistics* (3rd ed.) Reading, Mass.: McGraw-Hill, Inc., with kind permission of the publisher.

**Table 3b** *Critical values of* U *for a one-tailed test at 0.05; two-tailed test at 0.10\* (Mann–Whitney)*

$n_1$

| $n_2$ | 20 | 19 | 18 | 17 | 16 | 15 | 14 | 13 | 12 | 11 | 10 | 9 | 8 | 7 | 6 | 5 | 4 | 3 | 2 | 1 |
|---|---|---|---|---|---|---|---|---|---|---|---|---|---|---|---|---|---|---|---|---|
| 1 | 0 | 0 | – | – | – | – | – | – | – | – | – | – | – | – | – | – | – | – | – | – |
| 2 | 4 | 4 | 4 | 3 | 3 | 3 | 2 | 2 | 2 | 1 | 1 | 1 | 1 | 0 | 0 | 0 | – | – | – | – |
| 3 | 11 | 10 | 9 | 9 | 8 | 7 | 7 | 6 | 5 | 5 | 4 | 3 | 3 | 2 | 2 | 1 | 0 | 0 | – | – |
| 4 | 18 | 17 | 16 | 15 | 14 | 12 | 11 | 10 | 9 | 8 | 7 | 6 | 5 | 4 | 3 | 2 | 1 | 0 | – | – |
| 5 | 25 | 23 | 22 | 20 | 19 | 18 | 16 | 15 | 13 | 12 | 11 | 9 | 8 | 6 | 5 | 4 | 2 | 1 | 0 | – |
| 6 | 32 | 30 | 28 | 26 | 25 | 23 | 21 | 19 | 17 | 16 | 14 | 12 | 10 | 8 | 7 | 5 | 3 | 2 | 0 | – |
| 7 | 39 | 37 | 35 | 33 | 30 | 28 | 26 | 24 | 21 | 19 | 17 | 15 | 13 | 11 | 8 | 6 | 4 | 2 | 0 | – |
| 8 | 47 | 44 | 41 | 39 | 36 | 33 | 31 | 28 | 26 | 23 | 20 | 18 | 15 | 13 | 10 | 8 | 5 | 3 | 1 | – |
| 9 | 54 | 51 | 48 | 45 | 42 | 39 | 36 | 33 | 30 | 27 | 24 | 21 | 18 | 15 | 12 | 9 | 6 | 3 | 1 | – |
| 10 | 62 | 58 | 55 | 51 | 48 | 44 | 41 | 37 | 34 | 31 | 27 | 24 | 20 | 17 | 14 | 11 | 7 | 4 | 1 | – |
| 11 | 69 | 65 | 61 | 57 | 54 | 50 | 46 | 42 | 38 | 34 | 31 | 27 | 23 | 19 | 16 | 12 | 8 | 5 | 1 | – |
| 12 | 77 | 72 | 68 | 64 | 60 | 55 | 51 | 47 | 42 | 38 | 34 | 30 | 26 | 21 | 17 | 13 | 9 | 5 | 2 | – |
| 13 | 84 | 80 | 75 | 70 | 65 | 61 | 56 | 51 | 47 | 42 | 37 | 33 | 28 | 24 | 19 | 15 | 10 | 6 | 2 | – |
| 14 | 92 | 87 | 82 | 77 | 71 | 66 | 61 | 56 | 51 | 46 | 41 | 36 | 31 | 26 | 21 | 16 | 11 | 7 | 2 | – |
| 15 | 100 | 94 | 88 | 83 | 77 | 72 | 66 | 61 | 55 | 50 | 44 | 39 | 33 | 28 | 23 | 18 | 12 | 7 | 3 | – |
| 16 | 107 | 101 | 95 | 89 | 83 | 77 | 71 | 65 | 60 | 54 | 48 | 42 | 36 | 30 | 25 | 19 | 14 | 8 | 3 | – |
| 17 | 115 | 109 | 102 | 96 | 89 | 83 | 77 | 70 | 64 | 57 | 51 | 45 | 39 | 33 | 26 | 20 | 15 | 9 | 3 | – |
| 18 | 123 | 116 | 109 | 102 | 95 | 88 | 82 | 75 | 68 | 61 | 55 | 48 | 41 | 35 | 28 | 22 | 16 | 9 | 4 | – |
| 19 | 130 | 123 | 116 | 109 | 101 | 94 | 87 | 80 | 72 | 65 | 58 | 51 | 44 | 37 | 30 | 23 | 17 | 10 | 4 | 0 |
| 20 | 138 | 130 | 123 | 115 | 107 | 100 | 92 | 84 | 77 | 69 | 62 | 54 | 47 | 39 | 32 | 25 | 18 | 11 | 4 | 0 |

\* Dashes in the body of the table indicate that no decision is possible at the stated level of significance.

For any $n_1$ and $n_2$ the observed value of $U$ is significant at a given level of significance if it is *equal* to or *less* than the critical values shown.

SOURCE: R. Runyon and A. Haber (1976) *Fundamentals of Behavioural Statistics* (3rd ed.) Reading, Mass.: McGraw-Hill, Inc., with kind permission of the publisher.

## Table 4 — Critical values of $\chi^2$

| | Level of significance for a one tailed-test | | | | | |
|---|---|---|---|---|---|---|
| | 0.10 | 0.05 | 0.025 | 0.01 | 0.005 | 0.0005 |
| | Level of significance for a two-tailed test | | | | | |
| df | 0.20 | 0.10 | 0.05 | 0.02 | 0.01 | 0.001 |
| 1 | 1.64 | 2.71 | 3.84 | 5.41 | 6.64 | 10.83 |
| 2 | 3.22 | 4.60 | 5.99 | 7.82 | 9.21 | 13.82 |
| 3 | 4.64 | 6.25 | 7.82 | 9.84 | 11.34 | 16.27 |
| 4 | 5.99 | 7.78 | 9.49 | 11.67 | 13.28 | 18.46 |
| 5 | 7.29 | 9.24 | 11.07 | 13.39 | 15.09 | 20.52 |
| 6 | 8.56 | 10.64 | 12.59 | 15.03 | 16.81 | 22.46 |
| 7 | 9.80 | 12.02 | 14.07 | 16.62 | 18.48 | 24.32 |
| 8 | 11.03 | 13.36 | 15.51 | 18.17 | 20.09 | 26.12 |
| 9 | 12.24 | 14.68 | 16.92 | 19.68 | 21.67 | 27.88 |
| 10 | 13.44 | 15.99 | 18.31 | 21.16 | 23.21 | 29.59 |
| 11 | 14.63 | 17.28 | 19.68 | 22.62 | 24.72 | 31.26 |
| 12 | 15.81 | 18.55 | 21.03 | 24.05 | 26.22 | 32.91 |
| 13 | 16.98 | 19.81 | 22..36 | 25.47 | 27.69 | 34.53 |
| 14 | 18.15 | 21.06 | 23.68 | 26.87 | 29.14 | 36.12 |
| 15 | 19.31 | 22.31 | 25.00 | 28.26 | 30.58 | 37.70 |
| 16 | 20.46 | 23.54 | 26.30 | 29.63 | 32.00 | 39.29 |
| 17 | 21.62 | 24.77 | 27.59 | 31.00 | 33.41 | 40.75 |
| 18 | 22.76 | 25.99 | 28.87 | 32.35 | 34.80 | 42.31 |
| 19 | 23.90 | 27.20 | 30.14 | 33.69 | 36.19 | 43.82 |
| 20 | 25.04 | 28.41 | 31.41 | 35.02 | 37.57 | 45.32 |
| 21 | 26.17 | 29.62 | 32.67 | 36.34 | 38.93 | 46.80 |
| 22 | 27.30 | 30.81 | 33.92 | 37.66 | 40.29 | 48.27 |
| 23 | 28.43 | 32.01 | 35.17 | 38.97 | 41.64 | 49.73 |
| 24 | 29.55 | 33.20 | 36.42 | 40.27 | 42.98 | 51.18 |
| 25 | 30.68 | 34.38 | 37.65 | 41.57 | 44.31 | 52.62 |
| 26 | 31.80 | 35.56 | 38.88 | 42.86 | 45.64 | 54.05 |
| 27 | 32.91 | 36.74 | 40.11 | 44.14 | 46.96 | 55.48 |
| 28 | 34.03 | 37.92 | 41.34 | 45.42 | 48.28 | 56.89 |
| 29 | 35.14 | 39.09 | 42.69 | 49.69 | 49.59 | 58.30 |
| 30 | 36.25 | 40.26 | 43.77 | 47.96 | 50.89 | 59.70 |
| 32 | 38.47 | 42.59 | 46.19 | 50.49 | 53.49 | 62.49 |
| 34 | 40.68 | 44.90 | 48.60 | 53.00 | 56.06 | 65.25 |
| 36 | 42.88 | 47.21 | 51.00 | 55.49 | 58.62 | 67.99 |
| 38 | 45.08 | 49.51 | 53.38 | 57.97 | 61.16 | 70.70 |
| 40 | 47.27 | 51.81 | 55.76 | 60.44 | 63.69 | 73.40 |
| 44 | 51.64 | 56.37 | 60.48 | 65.34 | 68.71 | 78.75 |
| 48 | 55.99 | 60.91 | 65.17 | 70.20 | 73.68 | 84.04 |
| 52 | 60.33 | 65.42 | 69.83 | 75.02 | 78.62 | 89.27 |
| 56 | 64.66 | 69.92 | 74.47 | 79.82 | 83.51 | 94.46 |
| 60 | 68.97 | 74.40 | 79.08 | 84.58 | 88.38 | 99.61 |

Calculated value of $\chi^2$ must EQUAL or EXCEED the table (critical) values for significance at the level shown.
Abridged from R. A. Fisher and F. Yates, *Statistical Tables for Biological, Agricultural and Medical Research* (6th ed.) Longman Group UK Ltd (1974).

**Table 5** *Critical values of* t

| | Level of significance for a one-tailed test | | | |
| --- | --- | --- | --- | --- |
| | 0.05 | 0.025 | 0.01 | 0.005 |
| | Level of significance for a two-tailed test | | | |
| Degrees of freedom | 0.10 | 0.05 | 0.02 | 0.01 |
| 1 | 6.314 | 12.706 | 31.821 | 63.657 |
| 2 | 2.920 | 4.303 | 6.965 | 9.925 |
| 3 | 2.353 | 3.182 | 4.541 | 5.841 |
| 4 | 2.132 | 2.776 | 3.747 | 4.604 |
| 5 | 2.015 | 2.571 | 3.365 | 4.032 |
| 6 | 1.943 | 2.447 | 3.143 | 3.707 |
| 7 | 1.895 | 2.365 | 2.998 | 3.499 |
| 8 | 1.860 | 2.306 | 2.896 | 3.355 |
| 9 | 1.833 | 2.262 | 2.821 | 3.250 |
| 10 | 1.812 | 2.228 | 2.764 | 3.169 |
| 11 | 1.796 | 2.201 | 2.718 | 3.106 |
| 12 | 1.782 | 2.179 | 2.681 | 3.055 |
| 13 | 1.771 | 2.160 | 2.650 | 3.012 |
| 14 | 1.761 | 2.145 | 2.624 | 2.977 |
| 15 | 1.753 | 2.131 | 2.602 | 2.947 |
| 16 | 1.746 | 2.120 | 2.583 | 2.921 |
| 17 | 1.740 | 2.110 | 2.567 | 2.898 |
| 18 | 1.734 | 2.101 | 2.552 | 2.878 |
| 19 | 1.729 | 2.093 | 2.539 | 2.861 |
| 20 | 1.725 | 2.086 | 2.528 | 2.845 |
| 21 | 1.721 | 2.080 | 2.518 | 2.831 |
| 22 | 1.717 | 2.074 | 2.508 | 2.819 |
| 23 | 1.714 | 2.069 | 2.500 | 2.807 |
| 24 | 1.711 | 2.064 | 2.492 | 2.797 |
| 25 | 1.708 | 2.060 | 2.485 | 2.787 |
| 26 | 1.706 | 2.056 | 2.479 | 2.779 |
| 27 | 1.703 | 2.052 | 2.473 | 2.771 |
| 28 | 1.701 | 2.048 | 2.467 | 2.763 |
| 29 | 1.699 | 2.045 | 2.462 | 2.756 |
| 30 | 1.697 | 2.042 | 2.457 | 2.750 |
| 40 | 1.684 | 2.021 | 2.423 | 2.704 |
| 60 | 1.671 | 2.000 | 2.390 | 2.660 |
| 120 | 1.658 | 1.980 | 2.358 | 2.617 |
| ∞ | 1.645 | 1.960 | 2.326 | 2.576 |

Calculated *t* must EQUAL OR EXCEED the table (critical) value for significance at the level shown.

SOURCE: Abridged from R.A. Fisher and F. Yates, *Statistical Tables for Biological Agricultural and Medical Research* (6th ed.) Longman Group UK Ltd (1974)

**Table 6** *Critical values of Spearman's rho ($r_s$)*

| | Level of significance for a two-tailed test | | | |
|---|---|---|---|---|
| | 0.10 | 0.05 | 0.02 | 0.01 |
| | Level of significance for a one-tailed test | | | |
| | 0.05 | 0.025 | 0.01 | 0.005 |
| $n = 4$ | 1.000 | | | |
| 5 | 0.900 | 1.000 | 1.000 | |
| 6 | 0.829 | 0.886 | 0.943 | 1.000 |
| 7 | 0.714 | 0.786 | 0.893 | 0.929 |
| 8 | 0.643 | 0.738 | 0.833 | 0.881 |
| 9 | 0.600 | 0.700 | 0.783 | 0.833 |
| 10 | 0.564 | 0.648 | 0.745 | 0.794 |
| 11 | 0.536 | 0.618 | 0.709 | 0.755 |
| 12 | 0.503 | 0.587 | 0.671 | 0.727 |
| 13 | 0.484 | 0.560 | 0.648 | 0.703 |
| 14 | 0.464 | 0.538 | 0.622 | 0.675 |
| 15 | 0.443 | 0.521 | 0.604 | 0.654 |
| 16 | 0.429 | 0.503 | 0.582 | 0.635 |
| 17 | 0.414 | 0.485 | 0.566 | 0.615 |
| 18 | 0.401 | 0.472 | 0.550 | 0.600 |
| 19 | 0.391 | 0.460 | 0.535 | 0.584 |
| 20 | 0.380 | 0.447 | 0.520 | 0.570 |
| 21 | 0.370 | 0.435 | 0.508 | 0.556 |
| 22 | 0.361 | 0.425 | 0.496 | 0.544 |
| 23 | 0.353 | 0.415 | 0.486 | 0.532 |
| 24 | 0.344 | 0.406 | 0.476 | 0.521 |
| 25 | 0.337 | 0.398 | 0.466 | 0.511 |
| 26 | 0.331 | 0.390 | 0.457 | 0.501 |
| 27 | 0.324 | 0.382 | 0.448 | 0.491 |
| 28 | 0.317 | 0.375 | 0.440 | 0.483 |
| 29 | 0.312 | 0.368 | 0.433 | 0.475 |
| 30 | 0.306 | 0.362 | 0.425 | 0.467 |

For $n > 30$, the significance of $r_s$ can be tested by using the formula:

$$t = r_s \sqrt{\left(\frac{n-2}{1-r_s^2}\right)} \quad df = n - 2$$

and checking the value of $t$ in table 5.

Calculated $r_s$ must EQUAL or EXCEED the table (critical) value for significance at the level shown.

SOURCE: J.H. Zhar, Significance testing of the Spearman Rank Correlation Coefficient, *Journal of the American Statistical Association*, 67, 578–80. With the kind permission of the publishers.

**Table 7** *Critical values of Pearson's* r

| df | Level of significance for a one-tailed test | | | |
|---|---|---|---|---|
| | 0.05 | 0.025 | 0.005 | 0.0005 |
| df | Level of significance for a two-tailed test | | | |
| (N – 2) | 0.10 | 0.05 | 0.01 | 0.001 |
| 2 | 0.9000 | 0.9500 | 0.9900 | 0.9999 |
| 3 | 0.805 | 0.878 | 0.9587 | 0.9911 |
| 4 | 0.729 | 0.811 | 0.9172 | 0.9741 |
| 5 | 0.669 | 0.754 | 0.875 | 0.9509 |
| 6 | 0.621 | 0.707 | 0.834 | 0.9241 |
| 7 | 0.582 | 0.666 | 0.798 | 0.898 |
| 8 | 0.549 | 0.632 | 0.765 | 0.872 |
| 9 | 0.521 | 0.602 | 0.735 | 0.847 |
| 10 | 0.497 | 0.576 | 0.708 | 0.823 |
| 11 | 0.476 | 0.553 | 0.684 | 0.801 |
| 12 | 0.475 | 0.532 | 0.661 | 0.780 |
| 13 | 0.441 | 0.514 | 0.641 | 0.760 |
| 14 | 0.426 | 0.497 | 0.623 | 0.742 |
| 15 | 0.412 | 0.482 | 0.606 | 0.725 |
| 16 | 0.400 | 0.468 | 0.590 | 0.708 |
| 17 | 0.389 | 0.456 | 0.575 | 0.693 |
| 18 | 0.378 | 0.444 | 0.561 | 0.679 |
| 19 | 0.369 | 0.433 | 0.549 | 0.665 |
| 20 | 0.360 | 0.423 | 0.537 | 0.652 |
| 25 | 0.323 | 0.381 | 0.487 | 0.597 |
| 30 | 0.296 | 0.349 | 0.449 | 0.554 |
| 35 | 0.275 | 0.325 | 0.418 | 0.519 |
| 40 | 0.257 | 0.304 | 0.393 | 0.490 |
| 45 | 0.243 | 0.288 | 0.372 | 0.465 |
| 50 | 0.231 | 0.273 | 0.354 | 0.443 |
| 60 | 0.211 | 0.250 | 0.325 | 0.408 |
| 70 | 0.195 | 0.232 | 0.302 | 0.380 |
| 80 | 0.183 | 0.217 | 0.283 | 0.357 |
| 90 | 0.173 | 0.205 | 0.267 | 0.338 |
| 100 | 0.164 | 0.195 | 0.254 | 0.321 |

Calculated r must EQUAL or EXCEED the table (critical) value for significance at the level shown.
SOURCE: F.C. Powell, *Cambridge Mathematical and Statistical Tables*, Cambridge University Press (1976). With kind permission of the publishers.

## Table 8 *Random numbers*

| | | | | |
|---|---|---|---|---|
| 03 47 43 73 86 | 39 96 47 36 61 | 46 98 63 71 62 | 33 26 16 80 45 | 60 11 14 10 95 |
| 97 74 24 67 62 | 42 81 14 57 20 | 42 53 32 37 32 | 27 07 36 07 51 | 24 51 79 89 73 |
| 16 76 62 27 66 | 56 50 26 71 07 | 32 90 79 78 53 | 13 55 38 58 59 | 88 97 54 14 10 |
| 12 56 85 99 26 | 96 96 68 27 31 | 05 03 72 93 15 | 57 12 10 14 21 | 88 26 49 81 76 |
| 55 59 56 35 64 | 38 54 82 46 22 | 31 62 43 09 90 | 06 18 44 32 53 | 23 83 01 30 30 |
| 16 22 77 94 39 | 49 54 43 54 82 | 17 37 93 23 78 | 87 35 20 96 43 | 84 26 34 91 64 |
| 84 42 17 53 31 | 57 24 55 06 88 | 77 04 74 47 67 | 21 76 33 50 25 | 83 92 12 06 76 |
| 63 01 63 78 59 | 16 95 55 67 19 | 98 10 50 71 75 | 12 86 73 58 07 | 44 39 52 38 79 |
| 33 21 12 34 29 | 78 64 56 07 82 | 52 42 07 44 38 | 15 51 00 13 42 | 99 66 02 79 54 |
| 57 60 86 32 44 | 09 47 27 96 54 | 49 17 46 09 62 | 90 52 84 77 27 | 08 02 73 43 28 |
| 18 18 07 92 46 | 44 17 16 58 09 | 79 83 86 16 62 | 06 76 50 03 10 | 55 23 64 05 05 |
| 26 62 38 97 75 | 84 16 07 44 99 | 83 11 46 32 24 | 20 14 85 88 45 | 10 93 72 88 71 |
| 23 42 40 64 74 | 82 97 77 77 81 | 07 45 32 14 08 | 32 98 94 07 72 | 93 85 79 10 75 |
| 52 36 28 19 95 | 50 92 26 11 97 | 00 56 76 31 38 | 80 22 02 53 53 | 86 60 42 04 53 |
| 37 85 94 35 12 | 83 39 50 08 30 | 42 34 07 96 88 | 54 42 06 87 98 | 35 85 29 48 38 |
| 70 29 17 12 13 | 40 33 20 38 26 | 13 89 51 03 74 | 17 76 37 13 04 | 07 74 21 19 30 |
| 56 62 18 37 35 | 96 83 50 87 75 | 97 12 25 93 47 | 70 33 24 03 54 | 97 77 46 44 80 |
| 99 49 57 22 77 | 88 42 95 45 72 | 16 64 36 16 00 | 04 43 18 66 79 | 94 77 24 21 90 |
| 16 08 15 04 72 | 33 27 14 34 90 | 45 59 34 68 49 | 12 72 07 34 45 | 99 27 72 95 14 |
| 31 16 93 32 43 | 50 27 89 87 19 | 20 15 37 00 49 | 52 85 66 60 44 | 38 68 88 11 80 |
| 68 34 30 13 70 | 55 74 30 77 40 | 44 22 78 84 26 | 04 33 46 09 52 | 68 07 97 06 57 |
| 74 57 25 65 76 | 59 29 97 68 60 | 71 91 38 67 54 | 13 58 18 24 76 | 15 54 55 95 52 |
| 27 42 37 86 53 | 48 55 90 65 72 | 96 57 69 36 10 | 96 46 92 42 45 | 97 60 49 04 91 |
| 00 39 68 29 61 | 66 37 32 20 30 | 77 84 57 03 29 | 10 45 65 04 26 | 11 04 96 67 24 |
| 29 94 98 94 24 | 68 49 69 10 82 | 53 75 91 93 30 | 34 25 20 57 27 | 40 48 73 51 92 |
| 16 90 82 66 59 | 83 62 64 11 12 | 67 19 00 71 74 | 60 47 21 29 68 | 02 02 37 03 31 |
| 11 27 94 75 06 | 06 09 19 74 66 | 02 94 37 34 02 | 76 70 90 30 86 | 38 45 94 30 38 |
| 35 24 10 16 20 | 33 32 51 26 38 | 79 78 45 04 91 | 16 92 53 56 16 | 02 75 50 95 98 |
| 38 23 16 86 38 | 42 38 97 01 50 | 87 75 66 81 41 | 40 01 74 91 62 | 48 51 84 08 32 |
| 31 96 25 91 47 | 96 44 33 49 13 | 34 86 82 53 91 | 00 52 43 48 85 | 27 55 26 89 62 |
| 66 67 40 67 14 | 64 05 71 95 86 | 11 05 65 09 68 | 76 83 20 37 90 | 57 16 00 11 66 |
| 14 90 84 45 11 | 75 73 88 05 90 | 52 27 41 14 86 | 22 98 12 22 08 | 07 52 74 95 80 |
| 68 05 51 18 00 | 33 96 02 75 19 | 07 60 62 93 55 | 59 33 82 43 90 | 49 37 38 44 59 |
| 20 46 78 73 90 | 97 51 40 14 02 | 04 02 33 31 08 | 39 54 16 49 36 | 47 95 93 13 30 |
| 64 19 58 97 79 | 15 06 15 93 20 | 01 90 10 75 06 | 40 78 78 89 62 | 02 67 74 17 33 |
| 05 26 93 70 60 | 22 35 85 15 13 | 92 03 51 59 77 | 59 56 78 06 83 | 52 91 05 70 74 |
| 07 97 10 88 23 | 09 98 42 99 64 | 61 71 62 99 15 | 06 51 29 16 93 | 58 05 77 09 51 |
| 68 71 86 85 85 | 54 87 66 47 54 | 73 32 08 11 12 | 44 95 92 63 16 | 29 56 24 29 48 |
| 26 99 61 65 53 | 58 37 78 80 70 | 42 10 50 67 42 | 32 17 55 85 74 | 94 44 67 16 94 |
| 14 65 52 68 75 | 87 59 36 22 41 | 26 78 63 06 55 | 13 08 27 01 50 | 15 29 39 39 43 |

**Table 9** *z values and % of area under the normal curve*

The *z* scores below cut off the area stated between the score and the mean. e.g. a *z* of 1.65 cuts off 45.05% of the area above the mean leaving 4.95% to the extreme right of the normal distribution; a *z* score of −1.96 cuts off 47.5% of the area below the mean, leaving 2.5% to the extreme left.

| z | % | z | % | z | % | z | % | z | % | z | % |
|---|---|---|---|---|---|---|---|---|---|---|---|
| 0.01 | 0.40 | 0.51 | 19.50 | 1.01 | 34.38 | 1.51 | 43.45 | 2.01 | 47.78 | 2.51 | 49.40 |
| 0.02 | 0.80 | 0.52 | 19.85 | 1.02 | 34.61 | 1.52 | 43.57 | 2.02 | 47.83 | 2.52 | 49.41 |
| 0.03 | 1.20 | 0.53 | 20.19 | 1.03 | 34.85 | 1.53 | 43.70 | 2.03 | 47.88 | 2.53 | 49.43 |
| 0.04 | 1.60 | 0.54 | 20.54 | 1.04 | 35.08 | 1.54 | 43.82 | 2.04 | 47.93 | 2.54 | 49.45 |
| 0.05 | 1.99 | 0.55 | 20.88 | 1.05 | 35.31 | 1.55 | 43.94 | 2.05 | 47.98 | 2.55 | 49.46 |
| 0.06 | 2.39 | 0.56 | 21.23 | 1.06 | 35.54 | 1.56 | 44.06 | 2.06 | 48.03 | 2.56 | 49.48 |
| 0.07 | 2.79 | 0.57 | 21.57 | 1.07 | 35.77 | 1.57 | 44.18 | 2.07 | 48.08 | 2.57 | 49.49 |
| 0.08 | 3.19 | 0.58 | 21.90 | 1.08 | 35.99 | 1.58 | 44.29 | 2.08 | 48.12 | 2.58 | 49.51 |
| 0.09 | 3.59 | 0.59 | 22.24 | 1.09 | 36.21 | 1.59 | 44.41 | 2.09 | 48.17 | 2.59 | 49.52 |
| 0.10 | 3.98 | 0.60 | 22.57 | 1.10 | 36.43 | 1.60 | 44.52 | 2.10 | 48.21 | 2.60 | 49.53 |
| 0.11 | 4.38 | 0.61 | 22.91 | 1.11 | 36.65 | 1.61 | 44.63 | 2.11 | 48.26 | 2.61 | 49.55 |
| 0.12 | 4.78 | 0.62 | 23.24 | 1.12 | 36.86 | 1.62 | 44.74 | 2.12 | 48.30 | 2.62 | 49.56 |
| 0.13 | 5.17 | 0.63 | 23.57 | 1.13 | 37.08 | 1.63 | 44.84 | 2.13 | 48.34 | 2.63 | 49.57 |
| 0.14 | 5.57 | 0.64 | 23.89 | 1.14 | 37.29 | 1.64 | 44.95 | 2.14 | 48.38 | 2.64 | 49.59 |
| 0.15 | 5.96 | 0.65 | 24.22 | 1.15 | 37.49 | 1.65 | 45.05 | 2.15 | 48.42 | 2.65 | 49.60 |
| 0.16 | 6.36 | 0.66 | 24.54 | 1.16 | 37.70 | 1.66 | 45.15 | 2.16 | 48.46 | 2.66 | 49.61 |
| 0.17 | 6.75 | 0.67 | 24.86 | 1.17 | 37.90 | 1.67 | 45.25 | 2.17 | 48.50 | 2.67 | 49.62 |
| 0.18 | 7.14 | 0.68 | 25.17 | 1.18 | 38.10 | 1.68 | 45.35 | 2.18 | 48.54 | 2.68 | 49.63 |
| 0.19 | 7.53 | 0.69 | 25.49 | 1.19 | 38.30 | 1.69 | 45.45 | 2.19 | 48.57 | 2.69 | 49.64 |
| 0.20 | 7.93 | 0.70 | 25.80 | 1.20 | 38.49 | 1.70 | 45.54 | 2.20 | 48.61 | 2.70 | 49.65 |
| 0.21 | 8.32 | 0.71 | 26.11 | 1.21 | 38.69 | 1.71 | 45.64 | 2.21 | 48.64 | 2.71 | 49.66 |
| 0.22 | 8.71 | 0.72 | 26.42 | 1.22 | 38.88 | 1.72 | 45.73 | 2.22 | 48.68 | 2.72 | 49.67 |
| 0.23 | 9.10 | 0.73 | 26.73 | 1.23 | 39.07 | 1.73 | 45.82 | 2.23 | 48.71 | 2.73 | 49.68 |
| 0.24 | 9.48 | 0.74 | 27.04 | 1.24 | 39.25 | 1.74 | 45.91 | 2.24 | 48.75 | 2.74 | 49.69 |
| 0.25 | 9.87 | 0.75 | 27.34 | 1.25 | 39.44 | 1.75 | 45.99 | 2.25 | 48.78 | 2.75 | 49.70 |
| 0.26 | 10.26 | 0.76 | 27.64 | 1.26 | 39.62 | 1.76 | 46.08 | 2.26 | 48.81 | 2.76 | 49.71 |
| 0.27 | 10.64 | 0.77 | 27.94 | 1.27 | 39.80 | 1.77 | 46.16 | 2.27 | 48.84 | 2.77 | 49.72 |
| 0.28 | 11.03 | 0.78 | 28.23 | 1.28 | 39.97 | 1.78 | 46.25 | 2.28 | 48.87 | 2.78 | 49.73 |
| 0.29 | 11.41 | 0.79 | 28.52 | 1.29 | 40.15 | 1.79 | 46.33 | 2.29 | 48.90 | 2.79 | 49.74 |
| 0.30 | 11.79 | 0.80 | 28.81 | 1.30 | 40.32 | 1.80 | 46.41 | 2.30 | 48.93 | 2.80 | 49.74 |
| 0.31 | 12.17 | 0.81 | 29.10 | 1.31 | 40.49 | 1.81 | 46.49 | 2.31 | 48.96 | 2.81 | 49.75 |
| 0.32 | 12.55 | 0.82 | 29.39 | 1.32 | 40.66 | 1.82 | 46.56 | 2.32 | 48.98 | 2.82 | 49.76 |
| 0.33 | 12.93 | 0.83 | 29.67 | 1.33 | 40.82 | 1.83 | 46.64 | 2.33 | 49.01 | 2.83 | 49.77 |
| 0.34 | 13.31 | 0.84 | 29.95 | 1.34 | 40.99 | 1.84 | 46.71 | 2.34 | 49.04 | 2.84 | 49.77 |
| 0.35 | 13.68 | 0.85 | 30.23 | 1.35 | 41.15 | 1.85 | 46.78 | 2.35 | 49.06 | 2.85 | 49.78 |
| 0.36 | 14.06 | 0.86 | 30.51 | 1.36 | 41.31 | 1.86 | 46.83 | 2.36 | 49.09 | 2.86 | 49.79 |
| 0.37 | 14.43 | 0.87 | 30.78 | 1.37 | 41.47 | 1.87 | 46.93 | 2.37 | 49.11 | 2.87 | 49.79 |
| 0.38 | 14.80 | 0.88 | 31.06 | 1.38 | 41.62 | 1.88 | 46.99 | 2.38 | 49.13 | 2.88 | 49.80 |
| 0.39 | 15.17 | 0.89 | 31.33 | 1.39 | 41.77 | 1.89 | 47.06 | 2.39 | 49.16 | 2.89 | 49.81 |
| 0.40 | 15.54 | 0.90 | 31.59 | 1.40 | 41.92 | 1.90 | 47.13 | 2.40 | 49.18 | 2.90 | 49.81 |
| 0.41 | 15.91 | 0.91 | 31.86 | 1.41 | 42.07 | 1.91 | 47.19 | 2.41 | 49.20 | 2.91 | 49.82 |
| 0.42 | 16.28 | 0.92 | 32.12 | 1.42 | 42.22 | 1.92 | 47.26 | 2.42 | 49.22 | 2.92 | 49.82 |
| 0.43 | 16.64 | 0.93 | 32.38 | 1.43 | 42.36 | 1.93 | 47.32 | 2.43 | 49.25 | 2.93 | 49.83 |
| 0.44 | 17.00 | 0.94 | 32.64 | 1.44 | 42.51 | 1.94 | 47.38 | 2.44 | 49.27 | 2.94 | 49.84 |
| 0.45 | 17.36 | 0.95 | 32.89 | 1.45 | 42.65 | 1.95 | 47.44 | 2.45 | 49.29 | 2.95 | 49.84 |
| 0.46 | 17.72 | 0.96 | 33.15 | 1.46 | 42.79 | 1.96 | 47.50 | 2.46 | 49.31 | 2.96 | 49.85 |
| 0.47 | 18.08 | 0.97 | 33.40 | 1.47 | 42.92 | 1.97 | 47.56 | 2.47 | 49.32 | 2.97 | 49.85 |
| 0.48 | 18.44 | 0.98 | 33.65 | 1.48 | 43.06 | 1.98 | 47.61 | 2.48 | 49.34 | 2.98 | 49.86 |
| 0.49 | 18.79 | 0.99 | 33.89 | 1.49 | 43.19 | 1.99 | 47.67 | 2.49 | 49.36 | 2.99 | 49.86 |
| 0.50 | 19.15 | 1.00 | 34.13 | 1.50 | 43.32 | 2.00 | 47.72 | 2.50 | 49.38 | 3.00 | 49.87 |

# REFERENCES

ASCH, S.E. (1956) Studies of independence and submission to group pressure. 1. A minority of one against a unanimous majority. In *Psychological Monographs*, 70 (9) (Whole No. 416).

BANDURA, A. (1965 Influence of models' reinforcement contingencies on the acquisition of imitative responses. *Journal of Personality and Social Psychology*, 1, 589–95.

BRITISH PSYCHOLOGICAL SOCIETY (1992) *Ethical Principles for Conducting Research with Human Participants*. Leicester: BPS.

BRYMAN & BURGESS (eds) (1994) *Analysing Qualitative Data*. London: Routledge.

CARLSMITH, J. ELSWORTH, P. & ARONSON, E. (1976) *Methods of Research in Social Psychology*. Reading Mass': Addison–Wesley

CHARMAZ, K. (1995) Grounded theory, in Smith, J A, Harré R and Van Langenhove L (eds) *Rethinking Psychology*. London: Sage.

CIADINI. R.B. RENO, R.R. & KALLGREN, C.A. (1990) A focus theory of normative conduct: Recycling the concept of norms to reduce litter in public places. *Journal of Personality and Social Psychology*, 58, 1015–20.

COOLICAN, H. (1996) *Introduction to Research Methods and Statistics in Psychology* (Second edition). London: Hodder & Stoughton.

COOLICAN, H. (1999) *Research Methods and Statistics in Psychology* (Third edition). London: Hodder & Stoughton.

CUMBERBATCH, G. (1990) *Television Advertising and Sex Role Stereotyping: A Content Analysis* (working paper IV for the Broadcasting Standards Council), Communications Research Group, Aston University.

EDEN, D. (1990) Pygmalion without interpersonal contrast effects: whole groups gain from raising manager expectations. *Journal of Applied Psychology*, 75(4), 394–398.

GRBICH, C. (1999) *Qualitative Research in Health*. St. Leonards, NSW, Aus: Sage.

GROSS, R, & MCILVEEN, R. (1999) *Perspectives in Psychology*. London: Hodder & Stoughton.

HAYES, N. (1997) *Doing Qualitative Analysis in Psychology*. Hove: Psychology Press.

HOFLING C.K., BROTZMAN, E., DALRYMPLE, S., GRAVES, N. AND PIERCE, C.M. (1996) An experimental study in nurse–physician relationships, *Journal of Nervous and Mental Disease*, 143, 171–80.

HOVEY, H.B. (1928) Effects of general distraction on the higher thought processes. *American Journal of Psychology*, 40, 585–91.

HUMPHREYS, L (1970) *Tearoom Trade*. Chicago: Aldine.

JONES, E. E. & SIGALL, H. (1971) The bogus pipeline: a new paradigm for measuring affect and attitude *Psychological Bulletin*, 76, 349–64.

KRAUT, R., PATTERSON, M., LUNDMARK, V., KIESLER, S., MUKOPHADHYAY, T. & SCHERLIS, W. (1998) Internet paradox: A social technology that reduces social involvement and psychological well-being. *American Psychologist*, 53, 9, 1017–1031.

LATANÉ, B. & DARLEY J.J. (1968) Group inhibition of bystander intervention in emergencies. *Journal of Personality and Social Psychology*, 10, 215–221.

LATANÉ, B. & DARLEY, J. M. (1976) *Help in a Crisis: Bystander Response to an Emergency*. Morristown, N.J.: General Learning Press.

LINCOLN, Y.S. & GUBA, E.G. (1985) *Naturalistic Enquiry*. London: Sage.

MILGRAM, S. (1974) *Obedience to Authority*. New York: Harper & Row.

ORNE, M.T. (1962) On the social psychology of the psychological experiment: with popular reference to demand characteristics and their implications. *American Psychologist*, 17, 776–83.

ORNE, M.T. & SCHEIBE, K.E. (1964) The contribution of non-deprivation factors in the production of sensory deprivation effects: The psychology of the 'panic button'. *Journal of Abnormal and Social Psychology*, 68, 3–12.

PIDGEON & HENWOOD (1997) Using grounded theory in psychological research, in Hayes, N. (Ed) *Doing Qualitative Analysis in Psychology*. Hove: Psychology Press.

PILIAVIN, I. M. RODIN, J. & PILIAVIN, J.A. (1969) Good samaritanism: an underground phenomenon? *Journal of Personality and Social Psychology*, 13, 289–99.

RACHEL, J. (1996) Ethnography: practical implementation in Richardson, J.T.E. (Ed) *Handbook of Qualitative Research Methods for Psychology and the Social Sciences*. Leicester: BPS Books.

RICHARDSON, J.T.E. (ED) (1996) *Handbook of Qualitative Research Methods for Psychology and the Social Sciences*. Leicester: BPS Books.

ROETHLISBERGER, F.J. & DICKSON, W.J. (1939) *Management and the Worker*. Cambridge, Mass: Harvard University Press.

ROSENTHAL, R. (1966) Covert communication in the psychological experiment. *Psychological Bulletin*, 67, 356–67.

ROSENTHAL, R. & JACOBSON (1968) *Pygmalion in the Classroom*. New York: Holt.

ROSENTHAL. R. & LAWSON, R. (1964) A longitudinal study of the effects of experimenter bias on the operant conditioning of laboratory rats. *Journal of Psychiatric Research*, 2, 61–72.

ROSENTHAL, R. KOHN, P., GREENFIELD, P.M. & CAROTA, N. (1955) Experimenters' hypothesis–confirmation and mood as determinants of experimental results. *Perceptual and Motor Skills*, 20, 1237–1252.

ROSNOW, R.L. & ROSENTHAL, R. (1997) *People Studying People: Artifacts and ethics in behavioural research*. New York: W.H. Freeman.

SEARS, D. (1986) College sophomores in the laboratory: influences of a narrow database on social psychology's view of human nature. *Journal of Personality and Social Psychology*, 51, 515–30.

SMITH, J.A. (1995) Semi-structured interviewing and qualitative analysis. In Smith, J.A. Harré, R. & Van Langenhove, (Eds) *Rethinking Methods in Psychology*. London: Sage.

SMITH, P.B. & BOND, M.H. (1997) *Social Psychology Across Cultures: Analysis and Perspectives*. London: Harvester Wheatsheaf.

SPIELBERGER, C.D. GORSUCH, R.L. & LUSHENE, R.E. (1983) *Manual for the State–Trait Anxiety Inventory*. Palo Alto, Calif: Consulting Psychologist Press.

TUKEY, J.W. (1977) *Exploratory Data Analysis*. Reading Mass.: Addison–Wesley.

# INDEX

Note: page numbers in *italic* denote figures; page numbers in **bold** denote definitions or calculation procedures.